Help! I'm a WAHM

Stress Relief for Mothers Doing it All

Anita Marchesani, Ph.D.

Copyright © 2008 by Anita Marchesani, Ph.D.

ISBN: 978-0-6152-3688-9

All rights reserved. No part of this book may be reproduced by any mechanical, photographic, or electronic process.

The author of this book does not dispense medical or psychological advice. No attempt is made by the author to diagnose, treat, or manage any medical, psychological, or emotional condition. The author assumes no liability for actions taken by the reader during or after reading this book. The sole intention of the author is to provide general information that may assist the reader in understanding more about her/himself.

Cover art by Kristina Mentzer

Back cover photo courtesy of Maureen Cogan of MoCoPhoto (www.mocophoto.com)

Please visit www.dr-anita.com for more information about this author.

CONTENTS

Introduction... 5
    A Little Bit About Me.. 7
    A Peek at the Economics of Home Based Businesses............... 8
    Making the Most of This Workbook.. 9
    An Inspirational Place to Start... 10

Chapter 1 – What is Stress?.. 14

Chapter 2 – Why Worry About Stress?....................................... 19
    Physical Impact of Stress... 20
    Emotional and Behavioral Effects.. 23
    Summary of the Effects of Stress... 28

Chapter 3 – How Stressed Am I?.. 29
    Self Report Survey... 30
    The Meaning of the Scores.. 32

Chapter 4 – Let's Get Started!.. 33

Chapter 5 – Relieving the Fight or Flight Response 39
    The Power of Breath 39
    Relaxation Techniques 42
    Exercise 48

Chapter 6 – Is Your Mind Your Worst Enemy? 62
    The Tendency to Catastrophize 67
    The Nasty Words: "Should" and "Must" 69
    No More All-or-Nothing Thinking! 72
    Banishing Inappropriate Guilt 75
    The Problem With Multitasking 77

Chapter 7 – My Husband Doesn't Take My Business Seriously 81
    It Starts With You 82
    More Significant Spousal Concerns 85
    Is He Feeling Left Out? 87

Chapter 8 – Getting Control of Your Time 90
    The Email Dilemma 93
    What Happened to My Vacation Time??? 96
    The Power in Planning Time 97
    Embrace Delegating! 99

Chapter 9 – Seeing the Results 104

Introduction

In the midst of the debate between mothers who work outside the home and mothers who stay at home is lost a wonderful, yet under-estimated, lifestyle. They are mothers who run businesses from their homes, otherwise known as Work at Home Moms (WAHMs in internet lingo), and they refuse to compromise on important aspects of their lives. They lead fulfilling, challenging, and immensely rewarding lives, prioritizing their desire to be present in the lives of their children, while honoring a need to contribute to the economy of their families. What would it be like for you to both remain at home, and earn an income? Have you fantasized about it? Wistfully dreamed of having the best of all worlds? I'm here to tell you that you *can* have it all!

The good news is that you can have the best of all worlds. The not-so-good news is that the work at home lifestyle does bring challenges that other lifestyles don't have. While many services help you determine which business is best, encouraging you to jump in and share in the benefits and joys of working at home, precious few resources address the unique and specific stresses of WAHM's.

Another source of frustration with the WAHM situation is the general lack of societal understanding about what WAHMs do. There are magazines and publications to assist and support women who work outside the home, and there are organizations and books to support stay at home mothers (SAHMs). However, very few publications exist to address the WAHM's unique needs.

Why is it an issue? Well, one reason involves identity, and how WAHMs are perceived. If you meet someone for the first time, and you discover the woman stays at home with her children, you form a certain idea of this woman in your mind. This image of her stems from years of personal experience, media influence, and your own family experience. You might assume things about the educational background of this woman, perhaps believing her to be less ambitious and less business-minded.

On the other hand, if you meet a woman and find out she works outside the home in a salaried position, you also make assumptions about her. Again these would involve her educational background and level of overall motivation. Learning about her children, you would know that she probably utilized day care options at some point, and that she has to arrange for child care during the early school years. You may wonder how much time she spends with her children, particularly if she works in a high level, even executive, position.

Knowing that a stay at home mother also runs a home based business throws all prior assumptions out the window. Obviously this demonstrates a woman who wants to maintain a prominent role in the lives of her children, yet also take on the demanding role of entrepreneur. Neither of these roles is particularly easy, and although mothers who work outside the home face their own unique challenges, it seems that WAHMs might experience both the best, and the most challenging, of both worlds.

However, this complex lifestyle receives so little attention and support. As a result, the general population has a difficult time comprehending women who choose this life. From a personal standpoint, the WAHM can feel lost and ill-defined. She doesn't fit the stereotypical mold of the SAHM, but neither does she fit the standard ideas of a mother who works outside the home. When trying to recruit customers and clients, presenting themselves as "only" a business woman neglects an important part of who they are, but "only" focusing on the stay at home aspect marginalizes their critical economic and social contribution.

So, who exactly IS a WAHM? This lack of true identity results in misperceptions of what they do with their day, how available they are, how much they really dedicate to either their children or their career, and the fact that they are out to build businesses and make money.

In this workbook, I seek to help you identify these aspects of the work at home (WAH) lifestyle and learn ways to relieve some of the stress they can bring. We can't change the way society views us in the short term, but we can learn how to cope with the frustrations and challenges it can bring. In the pages to come, I will discuss briefly what stress is, why we need to learn ways to relieve and manage it, and then I will talk about steps you can take to create a less stressful way of being.

Apart from some challenges and aggravations, make no mistake about it: running your home-based business while also being a full time parent can be a viable option for many women. I know all of this first hand, because I run a home based business, while also homeschooling my two sons. And many of my clients engage in meaningful vocations from their homes, while prioritizing their family lives. The first step in relieving stress is to understand how special this lifestyle is, and that there are ways to help decrease the craziness and overwhelm. Others have learned techniques and made big improvements, and you can too.

A Little Bit About Me

Before I started my coaching practice from my house, I worked as a licensed psychologist, specializing in patients with chronic and acute medical problems. My job involved helping people experiencing chronic pain, heart disease, and cancer learn ways to cope with the emotional part of their illnesses.

After about 10 years working with this population, though, I realized I wanted to be at home with my children. I closed my therapy practice and took the additional step of bringing my boys home for education. I realize many of you will not make the homeschooling leap. But even if you send your children to school, starting life as a WAHM can be like landing on a different planet with no instructions on what to do once you arrive. At least that's how I felt when I started my home-based practice. No one taught me, in all my years of post-graduate psychology education, exactly *how* to run a business, let alone one from my house. And never mind how to also juggle parenthood on top of it all!

I managed to learn on the job, and as my practice grew, I found myself working with other moms who started home-based businesses. And guess what? They needed help balancing it all, too! My own personal experience taught me so much, and luckily I had an educational background that allowed me to figure out how to manage the stress that comes with the WAHM lifestyle. I started to pass this along to my coaching clients, helping them make positive differences in their lives. Over the years, I watched the trend of WAHM's grow and expand, allowing women to flourish and blossom without compromising that which was most important to them.

A Peek at the Economics of a Home Based Business

Despite the satisfying lifestyle of the WAHM, as I discussed a few pages ago, many people tend to overlook or discount it. For the most part, this lifestyle tends to be marginalized. There has been no research to back up my claims, but I routinely hear about women whose spouses, family members and friends fail to take their business seriously. Struggling to define one's self as a business owner, when the important people around you fail to see you as one, adds to stress. The fact that most people don't grasp the nitty-gritty of the WAHM life can add to overwhelm.

Before I start talking about relieving stress, I'd like to take a look at one segment of the economic power of WAHM's. Many women start businesses in a network marketing or direct sales company. These companies often sell merchandise during product parties or through word of mouth. The Washington, DC-based Direct Selling Association reported the following estimates of network marketing businesses for the year 2006:

- sales in the United States amounted to $32.8 billion for direct sales and network marketing businesses
- in-home sales accounted for almost 67% of the sales dollars
- 82% of the sellers were women
- 77% of the sellers fell into the 18 to 54 years age group (prime parenting years)
- just under 90% work less than 30 hours per week

Looking at these statistics, it is easy to see the economic and lifestyle power of work at home mothers who join network marketing or direct sales businesses. Not only does this segment of the economy show no signs of slowing down, these numbers don't even include the vast numbers of women who run home based businesses of their own creation. Picture all the women who sell their handmade jewelry, run a coaching practice (like yours truly!), do web design and marketing services, photography, interior design, and you get the idea. The sky is the limit for women who want to make money from their homes!

So we've established that women who start a home based business are neither alone, nor are they simply indulging a hobby. It is real money that exchanges hands, and real checks are flowing into the mailboxes of WAHM's every day. However, it is important to also take a look at the last statistic I reported – that is, most work at home moms do so part time. This should make sense, given the fact that the primary factor behind starting a home based business is to do something that fits in with their current family-oriented schedule. In most families, this would mean working part time hours.

Because they are working fewer hours, generally WAHM's incomes do not match that of full time workers. However, this should not minimize the impact of the income – after all, money is money, no matter how much, not to mention the tax advantages of working your own business.

But clearly the biggest economic impact of working at home is the ability to be more present in the lives of our children. This does translate directly into dollars when considering how much money you would have to pay someone to watch your children. WAHM's can schedule client meetings, product parties, networking meetings, and other work-related duties to coincide with child care and school. WAHM's do not have to worry as much about fluctuating school schedules and who will watch them if they are sick from school. And, you have no worries about the character and nature of the person spending time with your children!

Making the Most of This Workbook

As we move forward, I will ask direct questions and set forth specific issues to ponder. I have provided space in this workbook for you to write your responses, and I strongly encourage you to take advantage of this important step. The act of writing down significant issues can influence your life in profound ways, and you don't have to be a good writer in order to benefit! Writing your thoughts and feelings helps you clarify what is actually going on. Writing can be a type of meditation or prayer in which you give voice to the chatter that clutters your mind and clouds your thinking.

We all have thoughts all day long. We often act on these thoughts, whether it makes sense to or not. Part of the reason we act on our thoughts is that they become jumbled in our minds, they co-mingle with things that happened to us in the past, anxieties we have about the future, and misinterpretations about what is going on now. All these thoughts are swirling around inside your brain, with no real logic or structure to them.

Writing imposes structure on all these thoughts running around our heads. It forces us to refine what we want and what we need, what is real and what is imagined, what we hope and what we dream. If you do nothing else I suggest in this book, please do take the time to write your responses to my questions. The mere act of writing often leads to insights and clarity as you seek to improve your lifestyle.

Of course, if you prefer to create real change, you will find more specific advice and suggestions to relieve stress. Implementing these suggestions will be much easier if you have a more accurate understanding of your individual issues by writing about them. So, while answering the questions is not technically required, it will certainly add to the benefit you can gain from this book.

An Inspirational Place to Start

Before we start the process, I'd like to reinforce perhaps the most important principle to remember. Whether you are currently a WAHM, or are thinking of becoming a WAHM, you will face challenges. The glue that holds the core of your being together and will see you through good times and not-so-good times is in the reason you chose this lifestyle. In learning to better manage your demands, always come from the place within your heart that lead you along this path in the first place.

Take a few moments now to record in the following space the reason you started your home-based business, or the reason you are thinking of taking the plunge:

_____
_____
_____
_____
_____
_____
_____

This is your beacon, your guiding star.

Every single day, maybe even multiple times each day, I encourage you to remember *why* you decided to be a WAHM. Frequently re-read what you wrote in the above lines. Whether you struggle with entertaining a toddler, or with growing your client base, ground yourself by thinking of the events that brought you to be a WAHM. Remember your motivation, remember the big picture, and have faith in your decisions. There is tremendous power in the intimate relationship between working at home and mothering. Be confident that fulfillment and satisfaction can trump any obstacle. No one said it is easy, but *you can do it!* Keep your vision steady and unwavering, and you will find you can balance and achieve the joy you seek. And if you haven't yet developed a vision for your life, have no fear! You'll do just that in a few pages.

While I can say with confidence that I believe wholeheartedly in your ability to relieve the stress of the WAHM lifestyle, I'd also like to take a moment to set the stage for developing realistic expectations. I will not give you a sugar-coated version of stress management in this workbook. What do I mean by that? Well, if you live a stressful lifestyle right now, and you want relief, you have choices. One choice involves going to your doctor and requesting medication to alleviate your stress symptoms. While medications have changed some people's lives, and allow them to function because they become nonfunctional without the medications, for the average person, jumping to a pharmaceutical intervention is overkill. No pill can take away the impact of putting too much on your plate, and it can't teach you to say "no" to requests when you don't really want to do something. A pill can't prevent you from over-committing your time, nor can it help you manage your time more effectively.

So what's the other option? Simply put, you must change the way you do *some* things (not everything) in order to harness your stress level. The changes do not have to be major, sweeping changes. In fact, you will discover some of the strategies in this book can be rather easy. Other strategies might involve higher degrees of change. And you may even have to learn how to say "no." For some of you, that alone could be a monumental task! But I can promise you that the rewards for all of your hard work will make it worthwhile. Tackling your obstacles might mean the difference between giving up your dreams of being a WAHM, and keeping your dream alive.

I can't decide which changes might be best for you to make. Only you have that power of discernment. But the good news is, now that you own this book, it isn't going anywhere! In other words, if you find many things you would like to try but lack the energy to devote to such changes right now, realize that managing stress is a journey.

Stress relief is a work in progress. That means you can do a little now, and then return to do a little more in a few months. In many ways, this might be a preferable approach for most women. Integrate one or two strategies at a time, letting each one "sink in" until it becomes habitual. For some of the tactics I discuss, such as regular exercise (you didn't *really* think a legitimate book about relieving stress would *not* include exercise, did you?), focusing on one change at a time makes sense.

So grab a pencil and a cup of chamomile tea, put your mind in a receptive and optimistic state of mind, and dive in. Absorb what makes sense to you and resonates with you, and leave the rest for another time. Not every single item or issue will be relevant to your particular situation. Do not be surprised if you find yourself skipping over a section because it is an area of your life you have under control. On the other hand, you may discover a need to linger over some areas in the book, because they represent a "hot button" topic for you, or you have trouble generating ideas for tackling it.

All the strategies I introduce here have a great deal of quality research to back up my decision to include them. I don't talk about research in this book, but if you are interested in knowing more, please feel free to contact me for references.

Chapter 1 – What Is Stress?

What is the definition of *stress*?

Before I give you the answer, take a few moments to consider the following questions about how you experience stress in your life.

1. How do I, personally, define *stress*?

_____
_____
_____
_____
_____

2. How do I *know* when I am stressed? What changes do I notice?

_____
_____
_____
_____
_____
_____
_____

3. What are the effects of stress on my life? Does my stress level impact anyone else around me?

_____
_____
_____
_____

_____
_____
_____
_____
_____
_____
_____
_____
_____

Now that you have narrowed down how you experience stress in your life, compare it to what the experts say.

It might surprise you to know that researchers historically have had difficulty agreeing on a definition of stress. Without going into all the gory details, what you need to know is that stress is all about how an individual person *perceives* things around her.

For the sake of this workbook, we will use the following definition:

> *Stress is the perception that the demands placed on you exceed your perceived ability to meet those demands, with the resources you have at the moment.*

There are a number of important features of the definition that I would like to briefly highlight. One, the prominence of the word "perception" should jump out. As I mentioned previously, stress revolves around how someone *perceives* their situation, *not how the situation actually is*. This is perhaps the most important aspect in understanding stress, because it opens doors to managing stress using some relatively simple techniques. It also explains the vast individual differences that exist in how we cope with life events.

For some people, just the littlest thing can push them over the edge into major stress reaction. Other women seem to serenely juggle five children, twelve activities, homework, and a full time business without a hair out of place. Different people have different thresholds for frustration, for managing details, for interacting with our kids, for dealing with clients, and so on. One person's idea of having a busy schedule may seem to the next person like a simple walk in the park.

Here is a more concrete example of how changing our perspective on something can alter how we respond. Suppose you are driving down a highway in your area, one on which drivers zip around without apparent care for the other drivers on the road. There may be frequent tailgaters, lots of close calls, and a high volume of cars on a regular basis. Imagine yourself driving along this highway, humming your favorite tune.

Suddenly, seemingly out of nowhere, a driver races up beside you and cuts right in front of you, coming close to clipping your front bumper at 60 miles per hour.

What is the first thing that goes through your head in this circumstance? Record it here:

_____
_____
_____

Probably your reaction involved some choice words which may or may not have four letters. In your head, you may have thought something to the effect, "That so and so, who does he think he is? He almost killed me! What a jerk, what a loser, he doesn't deserve to be on the road – why doesn't someone take his drivers' license away?!?!" In response to these thoughts going through your head, you might find yourself gripping the steering wheel more tightly, maybe gritting your teeth, or tailgating the driver in revenge. These reactions could last for a long time after the incident, even up to the point of you arriving home in a frustrated and angry mood. Would you be more likely to have a shorter fuse when dealing with your children or spouse under these conditions?

I'd like to rewind our example above, returning to the calmer scene of you driving on the busy highway, humming your tune. Let's imagine that same driver races up beside you, cutting right in front of your car, almost clipping your bumper at 60 miles per hour. This time, rather than thinking, "What a jerk," you think to yourself, "I wonder if that man's wife is in labor?" Or, "I wonder if his child is in the emergency room somewhere?" Or, "Maybe she's a doctor and a patient somewhere is in dire need of his expertise."

Does thinking these things change how you *feel* about the event?

Perhaps you feel slightly less aggravated, the emotional edge of the event decreased substantially. You may still be concerned about the unsafe manner in which he drove, but the heightened emotional impact has lessened. In this circumstance, you feel less angry because you understand this driver may have had a *reason* for driving that way, a reason that if you or I had, we would be driving the same way. It feels less personal, less dangerous and random. It reminds us that we simply do not know with any certainty what motivates another person to behave in a certain way at any particular time.

Changing our *perception* of the event changes our emotional and behavioral reaction to the event. Situations in and of themselves do not produce emotional responses in people. An event does not poke a button inside us that makes us respond automatically with an out-of-control emotion. It may *seem* as if that happens, because most of us are not accustomed to analyzing emotions, but in fact it is our thoughts, our perceptions, our interpretations of events that cause our stress reaction, not the event itself.

The other part of the definition of stress revolves around the idea of resources to cope with the demands being placed on us. Particularly as a WAHM, the demands made on our time and space can come all day long, and from so many different places. We need to manage clients' needs, return phone calls and emails, prepare marketing strategies, update bookkeeping before tax time, manage inventory, arrange networking opportunities, attend meetings, plan meals, make doctors' appointments for yourself and the children (maybe even also for your husband), clean the house, do laundry, take the pets to the vet, call repair people for anything wrong in the house, call teachers to discuss children's school progress, pay household bills, arrange transportation for children's activities, pull children through homework after school, manage play dates for children, coordinate fundraising activities, make sure the children are bathed and get to sleep at a normal hour, talk with the spouse about his day and his challenges, communicate important household information to him, nurture your marriage by discussing non-household and child-related topics, and finally, get enough sleep.

If you are a homeschooling WAHM, you can add to that list: choosing the right curriculum that meets the needs of each of your children, making sure you meet the legal requirements for homeschooling in your state, structuring the day so that your kids engage in their learning activities, and shuttle them to their endless groups, co-ops, classes, and play dates.

In that huge list, you might notice an absence of self care activities. Exercise, stress management, social time with friends, and good 'ole fashioned zone-out time don't even make the list. You can see where the definition of stress fits into the WAHM lifestyle quite easily – we perceive that all these demands exceed our ability and resources to cope with them. Yet as we will see in the next chapter, controlling this stress becomes important not only for our peace of mind, but also for our physical, emotional, and behavioral health.

Chapter 2 – Why Worry About Stress?

One of your first questions about stress might sound something like, "Why should I even worry about it? Isn't stress a normal, and unavoidable, part of life? Isn't everyone else feeling this way, too?"

Well, yes and no. In October, 2007, The American Psychological Association released results of a survey indicating that one-third of Americans cope with "extreme stress," and even more report their stress levels have increased over the past five years. The survey also showed almost half of Americans believe that stress has a negative impact on their lives, both personal and professional. About a third of those surveyed said balancing work and family issues contributed towards much of their distress, and even more said stress causes them to have conflicts with people in their lives.

On a physical level, 77% of the respondents noticed bodily symptoms due to stress, including sleep problems, back pain, headaches, stomach/intestinal issues, fatigue, and tight muscles. Psychological symptoms included irritability, anxiety and nervousness, and feeling blue.

That's a lot of people feeling stressed and the effects of stress. Statistically, we could even say that feeling stressed is "normal," because the vast majority of people experience it. But while stress might be normal by the numbers, it is MOST DECIDEDLY not preferable!

Stress is not a benign condition. For whatever reason, people tend to believe that just because they experience something "in the mind," it therefore doesn't really have a true impact. It's as if people think elevated levels of stress have no impact beyond what they emotionally experience. Having worked with stressed people for my entire career, I can assure you that nothing is farther from the truth. Excessive stress has a direct, negative, and strong impact on physical, emotional, and behavioral health.

Let's take a brief look at the effects of stress in each area of your life, and what can happen if you delay or avoid relieving your stress.

<u>Physical Impact of Stress</u>

When we experience stress, our bodies change in dramatic and measurable ways. If you have access to a qualified biofeedback provider, you can actually see the effects of stress on your body. Biofeedback is a technology that allows us to measure certain physiological processes in our bodies, and then display those measurements on a computer screen (or some other visual or even auditory mechanism). You could be hooked up to biofeedback equipment while sitting in front of a computer screen showing you in real-time what is going on in your body. As you think about stressful things, you can watch on the screen how your body changes – how some things increase and others decrease.

So exactly what changes in our bodies? Your body reacts to stress in many ways, and I will mention just a few here. For starters, stress raises your heart rate, your blood pressure, and your muscle tension. Breathing becomes shallow, and you tend to take more rapid breaths. Your level of perspiration increases too, meaning you sweat more. The skin temperature in your hands and feet actually decreases as your arteries and capillaries constrict, shunting more blood away from your extremities and towards the major muscles in your body. The reduction in blood flow to the periphery of your body makes them colder.

You may have heard the phrase "cold, clammy hands" to describe what someone experiences when they feel nervous or stressed. The reason we experience cold, clammy hands is because of the decrease in blood flow to our hands (making our skin temperature decrease) and the increased perspiration rate (making our hands sweat, feeling wet or clammy).

While this physical description of stress makes it seem unpleasant, our bodies actually have a remarkably efficient reason for undergoing all the changes. The human body is designed to meet the physical stressors they encountered on a regular basis. Up until relatively recently in history (within the past 200 years or so), humans lived in conditions that exposed them to physical danger - animals would chase them, natural disasters would cause people to alter their environment to deal with the changes, and warring tribes would suddenly attack other tribes. All these situations forced people to physically defend themselves. When facing down a saber-toothed tiger or other threat, a person would have two basic choices – either fight the tiger, or flee from the situation as quickly as possible.

Regardless of which option the person would choose, he or she would need a large amount of physical and mental energy to either fight or flee. The changes that happen in the human body are specifically designed to provide our bodies with the energy for either option. Our hearts get ready by pumping blood faster to deliver more oxygen, our cardiovascular system makes sure that the bigger muscles (like those in the upper legs and arms) have more blood pumped to them, energizing them for action. Those same muscles start to tense up in anticipation of being called upon to perform at maximum capacity. These physical responses optimized chances for early humans' survival, whether they choose to defend themselves physically or run from the situation. As a result, the response our bodies have to stress, the stress response, is also referred to as the "fight or flight" response.

The beauty of the fight or flight design is that our bodies eventually return to normal after the physical release from the fight or flight response. We can relax, and our bodies can begin to store up reserves to prepare to meet the next threat. Our bodies were made to respond to stress in an intense, physical way.

Can you anticipate the problem with our modern day lifestyle and the stress response in our bodies? When you think about the major stresses in your life, are most of them life threatening, physical threats? I am guessing the answer is "no." Most of the stress we currently experience is mental, or lifestyle-related, as opposed to life-endangering. We see time, or lack thereof, as a stress as we rush from place to place. We cope with rush hour traffic, demanding family members, nosy neighbors, money concerns, and even relationship woes these days.

The problem is that our bodies do not know the difference between *life-threatening stress,* and *lifestyle stress.* Our bodies will react in the same exact way as if a wolf was bearing down on us about to devour us for his next meal. The same changes occur, and our bodies wait for us to discharge that accumulated stress by either fighting or fleeing. From a physiologic standpoint, our bodies need a physical release in order to adequately recover from stress. But because our lifestyle stresses don't require that type of coping (we don't run away at full speed from a traffic jam – although we may want to!), our bodies don't know what to do with the accumulated stress reaction. Compounding the problem is the chronic nature of lifestyle stress. Most of our stresses are lower in intensity, but continually happen most days of the week. Stress is no longer a "once and done" type of experience.

Without a deliberate and adequate way of counteracting the stress response in our bodies, we are setting ourselves up for major problems. Left unchallenged, this chronically stressed lifestyle takes a deep toll on the body. The physical consequences of unmanaged stress can run the gamut from mild to severe, and can build up over time resulting in some extreme problems.

At the milder end, increased stress levels make us more susceptible to illnesses like the common cold and the flu. Headaches, nuisance back pain, neck and shoulder tension, teeth grinding or clenching, dizziness, a racing heart, chest tightness, digestive issues like stomach pains and diarrhea, irritable bowel syndrome, allergies, sleep problems, and changes in appetite normally result from stress. The appetite changes often can result in an unintended weight loss or gain. And the sleep disturbances result in people feeling persistently fatigued and tired.

More severe physical problems include developing chest pain that mimics heart attacks. In extreme cases, people believe they are having a heart attack and go to the emergency room for immediate evaluation. Some estimates indicate that up to 55% of people who present to the ER with suspected heart attack actually are a victim of stress and anxiety.

Pain levels tend to increase the more people allow their stress to continue unabated. By far, most of the patients I saw while working as a therapist in a chronic pain clinic had a history of unrelenting stress, and rarely taking care of themselves. While the causes of chronic pain are multidimensional and diverse, there is a clear relationship between pain and a lifetime of failing to take adequate care of one's self. A life spent attending only to external demands to the exclusion of self care and even basic stress management wears the body down.

Eventually, existing in a chronic state of stress depletes the body's reserves. If we don't adequately refill and balance our reserves, our bodies will fail us when faced with additional stress. And so it starts to break down, starting with minor aches and pains, building to more severe pain conditions like fibromyalgia.

Continuing on to even more severe problems, stress is related to the development of high blood pressure and ultimately heart disease. Recent studies have found that people who manage stress better have higher blood levels of HDL, the so-called "good cholesterol." Some research even points to a possible relationship between stress and cancer. If you have diabetes, stress impacts how your body uses insulin, resulting in a variety of secondary problems including vision and circulation difficulties.

Are you experiencing any physical effects of stress? If so, list them here:

_____
_____
_____
_____

Emotional and Behavioral Effects

Obviously, stress impacts our physical body. But it also negatively influences our emotional well-being. Emotional issues often translate into maladaptive behaviors that can compound everything! Going back to our definition of stress (perceiving the demands being made on us exceed the resources we believe we have to meet those demands), chronic stress means we are continually feeling "behind schedule." It means that in our minds, we are constantly saying to ourselves something that resembles, "I just can't do it all, I can't handle everything in my life, one more thing on my plate and I'll lose it."

Do you say things like that to yourself? If so, list your comments here:

_____
_____
_____
_____
_____
_____
_____
_____

Can you imagine the toll it would take on your emotional health to constantly believe you are not good enough? Your self esteem would plummet, and self respect would go with it. What would happen if you said out loud to your children every day, "You just can't handle everything on your plate, you don't have what it takes to get it done, you can't possibly do all you have to do."

Would your children eventually *believe* that about themselves, hearing it all day long, everyday, from one of the most important people in their lives? Probably.

Would they start to feel down, depressed, perhaps even helpless or hopeless about their ability to accomplish anything? Probably.

Would you actually say those things to your children? Probably not, because you know the impact it would have on them and their emotional development.

Guess what? If you have those thoughts going through your head about yourself, you create just those emotional reactions. You wear yourself down emotionally every day. What rational person *wouldn't* feel down and depressed if they truly believed those things about themselves?

Depression is a major illness, and because the mind and the body are intimately linked, it impacts physical disease as well. More depressed people have higher risk of cardiovascular disease, take longer to recover from surgery, require more pain medication, and show less recovery than non-depressed post-surgical patients. So, not only does stress itself contribute to a worsening physical condition, it also increases the chance of emotional problems that themselves impact physical health.

Are you experiencing emotional consequences of stress? If so, list them here:
_____
_____
_____
_____
_____

The behaviors we choose to engage in typically result from the way we feel. For instance, if we are feeling angry, we are more likely act irritably towards people around us. Perhaps if we are aggravated about something our friend said to us, we might have a shorter fuse with our children, more quickly resorting to yelling at them for minor offenses. Or if we are in a particularly good mood, we might be more apt to act in a calmer manner when dealing with our children's transgressions. How we feel emotionally directly influences our behaviors.

How does stress fit into this? Well, when we are feeling overwhelmed and stretched too thin, we may have less tolerance for things. We are so involved in the millions of thoughts swirling in our heads and trying to figure out how we are going to meet all our obligations that we simply have no "mental room" left for aggravations. When those aggravations do happen (and they will happen when you are least ready to handle them), we might lash out, yell, or break down and cry. Or, we may internalize the aggravation, inwardly seething and stewing about the irritation, which of course compounds the amount of stress we feel.

Eventually, we may try to lessen those really unpleasant feelings. After all, there is only so much we can take before we have to blow off some steam. When we are stressed, we don't have lots of extra mental space and energy, so trying to find ways to relieve stress when you are FEELING quite stressed usually results in one thing – resorting to the methods you have done in the past to relieve stress. When we have fewer emotional resources available, we return to our default.

This might not be a problem if in the past you manage stress by going for a long workout, or schedule a spa day, or take a half hour meditation/relaxation time, or start to say "No" to requests being made of you. However, many people do not use those sorts of techniques. Instead, they engage in undesirable, or even downright unhealthy behaviors. Many might reach for something to eat when you feel stressed. This is extremely common (ice cream and chocolate are the top two food items for stressed folks), but obviously problematic in the long run.

Not only is weight gain a real possibility, but the food intake combined with the stress hormones your body secretes can wreak havoc on your insulin levels. Fatty and sugary foods will leave you feeling sluggish and/or with a "sugar low" when the short term effects wear off. How do you then cope with those unpleasant feelings? By eating more later on, because the immediate pay off is an instant lift in your energy and emotions. You can see how this sets up a vicious cycle of emotional ups and downs (not to mention the increasing numbers on the scale).

On the other end of the spectrum, some people cope with stress by eating less. And often weight loss is a signal of someone feeling stressed. Some of you might be reading this and thinking, "Well, what's wrong with that, I'd love to have that outcome!" While I understand that reaction and can appreciate the desire to maybe have something "positive" come out of being stressed, what happens physiologically to someone losing weight due to stress is not healthy. Usually they eat few calories overall, but the calories they ingest tend to be of a lower quality. They rely more on unhealthy foods. Their bodies are simply not receiving the nutrients they need in order to function under the best of circumstances. But under stressful conditions, the body requires even MORE nutrients to deal with the physiologic impact of stress. Denying the body these nutrients can result in a deterioration of the body's defenses, leaving it susceptible to infections and illnesses. As women, excessive stress combined with weight loss can even lead to cessation of the menstrual cycle, as the body desperately tries to cope.

Eating changes are one area of behavioral effects of stress. Another behavioral impact of stress is reliance on some other substance to make us feel better temporarily. Therefore, the use of alcohol, smoking, and drugs tends to increase when people are stressed. Drinking alcohol, smoking cigarettes, and using drugs all have the same effect – short term relief from whatever emotional experience the person is having. These substances are extremely effective with providing an escape from feelings pressure. In fact, they are so good at helping evade stress that people often become dependent on them to help them cope. The immediate and consuming sense of relief unfortunately reinforces their use of this undesirable coping strategy. It creates a reason to utilize the substance again in the future, because it is relatively easy to obtain and use. Perhaps you can see where it might set the groundwork for a future addiction problem.

On a lighter note, people engage in other behavioral coping strategies that can have unintended negative consequences. Stressed people tend to have many things going on at once. To handle those different things, they might end up driving too fast to get somewhere, or they might do things that could distract them from driving safely. Although talking on a cell phone while driving is ubiquitous, doing it while feeling really stressed creates more opportunity for problems. This is because the driver is most likely more mentally engaged with the phone conversation than the road, since probably the phone call is dealing with one of the issues causing the increased stress. How many times have you wedged in a phone conversation while driving just to help you accomplish more?

We also might tend to rely on fast food to help during stressful times. Not only is eating while driving a hazard, but the food we choose tends to lack adequate nutritional value. It's great that fast food chains have included more salads and healthier fare. However, you can't eat a salad while driving, and if you need to eat while you drive, you are most likely restricted to a burger of some sort.

Also, when we feel that our time is at a premium, that we have little to spare, one of the first things to go is any exercise program you might be on. I know how it is, I've been there myself. We might rationalize that exercise is disposable –since it only involves US and is for no one's benefit except OUR OWN, therefore, it MUST NOT COUNT, right? What kind of logic is that??? Enough said.

And one other behavior we alter in response to stress – sleep. After getting rid of exercise, where is the one other place we can "create" needed time? At night, of course! Have you ever stayed up late, night after night, just trying to get it all done?

Guess what? The body views lack of sleep as a form of stress, too. So compounding all the lifestyle stressors you have with depriving your body of the time it needs to rest, restore, and rejuvenate creates added fight or flight response. And so it goes…..

Do you find yourself changing your behavior due to stress? If you do, list here the behaviors you notice:

_____
_____
_____
_____
_____
_____

Summary of the Effects of Stress

Believe it or not, my brief overview of the effects of stress merely scratches the surface of the impact stress has on a person. Volumes have been written on the subject, and continue to be researched and written about to this day. Basically, stress impacts every area of humans because stress lives not only in your head, it lives in your body, it lives through your behavior, and it lives in your emotions.

Chapter 3 – How Stressed Am I?

Now that you have a good idea of the effects of stress on a person, the next step is to assess the level of stress you experience. You might find it a good idea to get a sense of how stressed you are right now, before you start to make any changes.

I designed the following self-report survey just as a guideline for understanding the level of stress you are experiencing. It is not a scientifically validated test, although it is based on scientific stress research. What that means is that you can't use it to diagnose anything. But it can give you a sense of what is going on right now with your stress level. It is merely a barometer of how your stress levels could be impacting your life. As you start to incorporate stress relief techniques, you can retake this self-report survey to note improvements.

If you are experiencing noticeable problems like those noted in the self-report survey, please consult a physician. While your symptoms may be caused by stress, it is also possible there is a medical explanation for your symptoms. Do not delay. Even if a medical issue is causing your symptoms, you can still benefit from learning stress relief techniques. In some cases, these techniques can even help relieve your medical symptoms.

Directions:

Consider each of the following stress-related symptoms, and indicate the degree to which the symptom currently bothers you. Only mark a symptom if it is a CHANGE from your normal, or baseline, level. In other words, if you have never been a great sleeper, then only indicate "sleeping problems" if your sleep issues have worsened recently.

For each item, rank the degree to which it is a problem on a scale of 0 to 5. A "1" represents a low level of problem and "5" indicating a severe problem. If the item poses no problems at all, write in "zero" (0).

Emotional Signs and Symptoms

1. I have trouble making decisions. _____
2. I feel overwhelmed more than normal. _____
3. I find myself feeling anxious or nervous. _____
4. I worry about things, including the future, more than I normally do. _____
5. I feel like crying more than I normally do/I cry more than I normally do. _____
6. I feel as if I am pulled in so many directions at once, and I can't get it all done. _____
7. I know I can't maintain this pace for a long period of time. _____

Subcategory score: _____ (add up the numbers you indicated for each emotional sign or symptom) Range: 0 - 35

Physical Signs and Symptoms

1. My sleeping habits have worsened (either needing more sleep, or having insomnia). _____
2. My weight has changed (either up or down), even though I wasn't trying to gain or lose. _____
3. My appetite has changed. _____
4. My muscles feel tense or tight. _____
5. I have headaches. _____
6. My back hurts. _____
7. I get more sicknesses (colds and other infections) lately. _____
8. I sometimes feel my heart racing in my chest. _____
9. I have found out my blood pressure is higher than desirable. _____

10. Sometimes I feel tightness in my chest (not related to a medical condition). _____
11. My hands get sweaty. _____
12. My hands and feet feel colder than normal. _____
13. I have stomach or digestive problems. _____

Subcategory Score: _____ (add up the numbers for each physical sign or symptom)

Range: 0 - 65

Behavioral Signs and Symptoms

1. I am eating more or less than I normally do (unrelated to an intentional effort to change my weight). _____
2. I am smoking more than I normally do. _____
3. I consume more alcohol than is typical for me. _____
4. I find I am late for things more than usual for me. _____
5. Lately I have been avoiding people and events because I am overwhelmed. _____
6. My ability to concentrate has changed for the worse. _____
7. I find I am more irritable with others than usual, and I am snapping at people for no good reason. _____
8. I'm not paying as much attention to my physical appearance as I typically do. _____
9. I am not meeting my household responsibilities. _____
10. I can't seem to relax at all. _____

Subcategory Score: _____ (add up the numbers for each behavioral sign or symptom)

Range: 0 - 50

Determine the Meaning of the Scores

For the Emotional Signs and Symptoms category, a score from 0 to 8 reflects a negligible to mild effect of stress. A score from 9 to 20 would indicate a more moderate impact of stress on your emotional well being, and a score of 21 or higher shows that stress is taking a more severe toll on your emotions.

For the Physical Signs and Symptoms category, a score from 0 to 20 indicates a negligible to mild effect of stress. A score from 21 to 40 generally shows a more moderate effect, and a score of 41 or higher reflects a very strong impact of stress on your physical health.

On the Behavioral Signs and Symptoms scale, a score from 0 to 18 is a little- to mild effect. Scoring between 19 and 30 is a moderate effect, and 31 or higher is a strong or severe effect of stress on your behavior.

Now, apart from the overall scores for each subcategory, if there are a handful of signs or symptoms you indicated and you realize stress plays a major role in their presence in your life, put a little "star" next to those items. You will want to pay particular attention to those signs as you move forward. Even if your overall scores don't decrease dramatically, big drops on just a few items is major progress.

Chapter 4 – Let's Get Started!

In Chapter 1, you listed areas in which stress impacts you, and the lives of those around you. In the previous chapter, you shed light on the more specific effects of stress in different areas of your life. Putting these pieces of information together probably highlights all the reasons why you want to develop better stress relief techniques!

But before talking about specific strategies, we need to first clarify where you hope to end up after you start implementing stress relief strategies. Why? Well, imagine you have a family vacation coming up, and the day comes when you are ready to leave. What would happen if you realized you had no idea of your family's intended destination? You would all wake up, jump in the car, and then what? You could just start driving, I suppose. You could randomly pick a road or direction and take off. But who knows where you would end up, and if you would even like where you go? Or you may even just spend the entire week wandering around various roads and paths, never really ending up anywhere. And how would you know what to pack to wear?

Sound ridiculous? Of course it is – we would never think of leaving for a vacation without knowing where we are going. That's crazy.

Yet every time we embark upon something in our lives, whether it is starting a new career, having a family, decorating a room, moving to a new area, or becoming a WAHM, we often fail to define the end point, the outcome we hope to achieve with the path we take. Imagine how much nicer a room you are decorating would look if you have a picture either in your head or in a magazine of how you want it to end up looking. Knowing what you want to create makes it easier to decorate – you have a guideline for choosing colors, you are more focused when shopping for furniture because a particular piece will either fit with your vision, or it won't.

Another reason to start with a vision is that the act of developing it actually can reduce stress! In general, people like a certain amount of structure. Some people prefer highly structured environments, and some prefer less structure. Regardless of the actual amount of structure, people do better with boundaries. Knowing the end point, defining what you work for on a daily basis, can relieve some pressure because it gives us a specific, known payoff for our efforts. Having a vision of what we want to ultimately achieve makes the journey so much easier.

As a coach, I always advise my clients to start with the end in mind. And so, I will encourage you to do that now – develop a vision of your end point, of what you want your life to actually *look and feel like*. I am not simply talking about a life managing stress. Include all aspects of your life. Imagine you have enough time to exercise, eat well, attend to household duties, call clients, go to networking events, et cetera. Have a complete and detailed view of your ideal life. Once you know where you want to go, you can start the process of making it happen.

In the following space, record your vision of your ideal life, making sure to include all important things such as self care activities, family activities, and business and networking events. You may need to complete this on a separate paper for more room.

_____
_____
_____
_____
_____
_____
_____

_____
_____
_____
_____
_____
_____
_____
_____
_____

I'd now like you to take a few moments to think about what your life would feel like if your stress were more under control. You may need to close your eyes in order to do this exercise, but do take the time to do it. Picture yourself as vividly as you can, feeling in control, managing stress and the demands of your life, increasing your health and your energy level.

Write about how you will *feel* when you find relief from your stress. How will your day to day experience be different from the way it is now? How will these new feelings differ from your feelings now? Do put some time into this exercise, because having a clear, well developed vision of where you want to go in terms of stress relief will help you enormously in your process. It pulls you away from the overwhelm of the present moment, and reminds you of a critical piece of information:

You have the ability to change and to feel more in control. And the work you do to get there will make it all worthwhile. So let's get started:

Describe what you will *feel* like when your stress is relieved:

_____
_____
_____
_____
_____
_____

_____
_____
_____
_____

Now that you have a clearer idea of how you want your life and your business to function together, it's time to begin assessing how your business and life are functioning currently. The goal here is to identify the gap between where you are now, and where you want to be.

In the best case scenario, you would take one week and record what you do with all of your time. You would write down exactly what activities you do, and when you do them. Although it consumes a bit of time, and does take some effort (mainly just to remember to write everything down!), it helps identify all the tasks you accomplish in a given week. You can also record all the things you wanted to accomplish but did not.

If you would prefer not to take a week off of your efforts to relieve stress, I certainly understand! If your motivation is high, it's hard to muster enthusiasm for an activity like this. So, an alternative would consist of simply recalling your daily activities for a week. If you make to-do lists regularly, reviewing them from the past week will obviously help. If you are not a list-maker, please put in a good amount of time accurately recalling your activities. Managing a schedule when you forgot to include attending a weekly, non-moveable meeting is maddening!

Rather than consuming many pages in the middle of this workbook with this information, please turn to the back of the book for blank space to record this data. When you write it down, make sure to note how much time it took to complete each task, including family and spouse time, and helping your children with homework.

Once you have completed this activity, tally up the number of hours you spent in the major categories in your life. For example:

How many hours did you spend on business-related duties?
_____

How many hours did you spend with your children and their activities?
_____

How many hours did you spend together as a family? _____

How many hours did you spend on self care (exercising, friend-time)?
_____

How many hours did you spend with just your spouse or partner?
_____

How many hours did you spend on other things? _____

Now, compare this to your ideal vision of your life. Are there any gaps between where you are now, and where you want to be? If so, where are these gaps? And how big are they? Record the differences here:

_____
_____
_____
_____
_____
_____

Some of you may find this exercise to be depressing – such a large gap between your vision and your current reality. Evaluate your gap, but don't be scared by it! Use it to inspire, it is a beacon for you to really milk your lifestyle for all it is worth. If this describes you, I will offer a few words of genuine encouragement.

First of all, return right now to the space in which you recorded the reasons you decided to start a work at home business as a mother. Read the passage you wrote, read it out loud, and then read it again. And read it even one more time if you need more inspiration.

You are doing something wonderful for your family. You are putting your children first, prioritizing their needs, while at the same time carving out a niche in this world for yourself. You contribute to the economy of your family while also feeling connected to a larger world around you that is separate from your family. You live your life on you YOUR terms, making decisions every day that put your family first, with the health and well being of your children foremost in your mind. Why undermine all of that because you feel overwhelmed, when with just a bit of effort each day, you can make your WAH lifestyle really work for you. What you do on a daily basis is to be celebrated and encouraged. And it is hard!

Don't despair! You absolutely have the ability to learn stress relief and be successful in everything you do. Hang with this program, give yourself a break, and have faith.

The first stress relief technique is something you can start doing right away, and you'll feel better almost instantly. Read on!

Chapter 5 – Relieving the Fight or Flight Response

The things I will talk about in this first section dealing with specific actions to reduce stress can actually be used by anyone under stress for any reason, not just from the WAHM lifestyle. While WAHM's certainly cope with unique challenges, some stress relief basics remain the same. And I'll talk about the latter in this chapter.

<u>The Power of Breath</u>

The first technique you are going to practice is perhaps the easiest to learn, and certainly the most versatile one you will ever encounter – deep breathing.

Deep breathing involves just what you probably think it does – deep, controlled breathing. Sounds simple, and it is, but there are a few guidelines to maximize the effectiveness of the breaths. The basis for its effectiveness lies in the physiology of stress. Remember back in Chapter 2 when I described the fight or flight response? One of the physical effects of stress is that breathing becomes shallow and rapid. Sometimes you might even find yourself holding your breath, not even paying attention to the fact that you aren't breathing.

To counteract the automatic tendency to breathe in a shallow and rapid way, instead you will breathe deeply and slowly. Because it is impossible to breathe both rapidly and deeply at the same time, it is impossible for the body to be in stress mode and relaxed mode simultaneously. You will find deep breathing to bring almost instant relief, because you are forcing your body to be the opposite of stressed by breathing in a way that opposes the stress-related breathing.

How do you breathe deeply for maximum effectiveness? Here are the guidelines:

1. Inhale slowly and deeply. To remind yourself to inhale slowly, count to 4 or 5 in your mind as you inhale. Breathe in until your lungs have filled to their capacity. If you can, try "belly breathing," or breathing so that you concentrate on engaging more muscles in your abdominal area. This has the effect of expanding your lung capacity, therefore bringing more oxygen in to your body.
2. Briefly hold your breath once you have completed the inhalation. Hold your breath for just about one second, and no longer.
3. Slowly exhale, releasing your breath in a controlled fashion, and at a rate that is slower than your inhale. For example, if you inhaled to a count of 5, try to exhale to a count of about 8. This will force you to breathe in a slow and controlled manner.
4. Repeat deep breathing at least 4 times, more if you have the time.

I give you the counting guidelines simply as a way to assist you in slowing your breathing down. Do not get caught up in the numbers, or in thinking that you "have" to count to a certain number in order for it to be "right." The numbers aren't important. They simply guide you to breathe more slowly. You can also sing a short song in your head to achieve the same result. For instance, you could sing "Row, Row, Row Your Boat" on the inhale, and the on the exhale, try to make it through the whole song. Or you don't need to count or sing at all, as long as you can control your breath.

Some people mistake a "sigh" for deep breathing. A sigh is not a deep breath, because generally people inhale and exhale more rapidly. It does tend to pull more oxygen in because people do breathe more deeply with a sigh, but its relative speed means it does not have the same physical impact as a true deep breath.

How can you use deep breathing? Well, you can use it anywhere, anytime! If you are aware of feeling pressure or overwhelm, stop and take a few deep breaths to get your body back under control. You can do deep breathing every time you sit at a red light. You can set an alarm clock and breathe deeply for one minute every hour. You can do 4 deep breaths every time you see the word "business" (or another word or visual trigger of your choice).

The beauty of deep breathing is in its flexibility. You can do it just once or twice and feel almost instant relief. Or you can sit with your eyes closed for 5 minutes and deep breathe the entire time for deeper levels of relief and relaxation.

Take a few moments and practice deep breathing. Just try it once or twice. Record anything you notice when you did it:

_____
_____
_____
_____

Now, take a few moments to think about how you would like to incorporate deep breathing into your life. I realize it seems simple, and therefore insignificant. I can assure you that nothing can be farther from the truth. Many books have been written on the power of deep breathing, and research shows it has immediate physiological effects on the body. Remember, it is impossible to both breathe rapidly and deeply at the same time, so it cannot be possible for your body to both stressed and relieved at the same time.

Identify at least one way in which you commit to yourself to use deep breathing in your life on a regular basis. Remember to write down a strategy to help you *remember* to do it!

I will do deep breathing:

_____
_____
_____
_____
_____

I will remind myself to do this deep breathing by:

_____
_____
_____
_____
_____
_____

Relaxation Techniques

Related to deep breathing is the next step in managing the physical impact of stress – relaxation techniques. Relaxation techniques refer to a wide range of procedures all designed to completely reverse the fight or flight response in the body. Just as it is impossible to breathe both rapidly and deeply at the same time, so it is also physiologically impossible to be both stressed and relaxed at the same time. Here's why:

Recall that during a stress response, the body reacts in predictable ways. The heart rate, blood pressure, muscle tension, and skin conductance (sweating) all increase, the skin temperature in your hands and feet decrease, and of course your breathing becomes more shallow and rapid. This is the stress reaction.

One way of relieving stress is to counteract these physical changes resulting from the fight or flight reaction. If we could decrease heart rate, blood pressure, muscle tension, increase peripheral skin temperature, and slow down breathing, we would have the opposite of stress. The opposite of stress is relaxation, and indeed it IS possible to reverse all those stress reactions and create a relaxation response. Being able to create the relaxation response guarantees stress relief, because it is physiologically impossible to have an elevated heart rate (like during stress) and a decrease in heart rate (like during relaxation) at the same time. So we can directly reduce stress by controlling these bodily reactions.

You may wonder if it is even possible to control things like heart rate and blood pressure. Until about 40 years ago, it was believed that these physiologic reactions were automatic and uncontrollable. We now know, through much scientific research and clinical experience, we CAN learn to control these reactions in our bodies, simply by using some behavioral and mental techniques.

These techniques are grouped into a big category referred to as *relaxation techniques*. There are many ways to achieve relaxation, and in fact there are no "right" or "wrong" techniques or approaches. I will talk about some basic characteristics of effective relaxation techniques. Beyond these, you can customize your own approach to this method, adding things you like and that help you deepen the relaxation response.

The ultimate goal of relaxation is to create an experience in which all the effects of stress on the body reverse themselves. If you had access to the biofeedback equipment I mentioned earlier in the book, you would be able to actually see your heart rate, blood pressure, and other measures go down as you relax more deeply. Mentally, you will also experience a sense of peace, relaxation, and calm. You will not be unconscious or unaware of anything, so that if you are relaxing while your child is napping and she wakes up calling for you, you will still hear her and respond. You will be aware of noises around you if there are any, but they will not disturb you or bother you.

Ideally, you would practice relaxation methods for 30 minutes each day. However, that amount of time might not be realistic for most WAHM's. Instead, I would suggest aiming for 15 minutes each day, and as you progress in your practice of relaxation, you might find you can achieve the same results in even less time, perhaps 10 minutes.

The actual method you use can vary. I will describe one method here that is a great place to start for folks who have never practiced relaxation before. As you work on achieving relaxation, please know that it is a skill, and just like any other skill you are trying to master, it may take time and effort to master the method. Without a doubt, the hardest part of learning to relax is learning to focus your attention on relaxation, preventing your mind from wandering to nonrelaxing thoughts. If you are thinking about anything but relaxation, like your grocery list, the clients you have to call, the tax forms you need to prepare, you will not be able to relax. Remember that relaxation and stress are incompatible – you cannot experience one when you are experiencing the other.

Learning to harness your mind to prevent it from wandering is easier for some than others. If, while you are trying to induce the relaxation response, you find your mind has wandered, gently refocus your attention on the task at hand, and don't chastise yourself for it. It is normal to have difficulty keeping your mind focused on relaxation, and you need to get in the habit and practice of concentrating on non-stress producing ideas.

When you start to relax, find a time when you are not going to be bothered by ringing phones, chattering children, or barking dogs. This is essential for your experience. You will need to either sit or lay down in a comfortable position, as you will be still for the length of the relaxation period. I know this might be a near-impossibility for mothers of young children, and if you cannot create the time and space to make this work on a regular basis, grab the time and opportunities when you can. It will be worth your while to develop this practice for future stress relief.

You can try some techniques to make it easier to focus your mind on relaxation and away from distractions. One thing to try is listening to peaceful, calming music during the process. You can enhance the effect by using headphones to listen to the music. The headphones function by filtering out extraneous noises, plus they allow you to hear the music in more pure form. Picking the right music sets the tone for your quest to turn down your mind's chatter and focus only on relaxing the body.

If music alone does not provide enough of a focal point to minimize mind-wandering, you can purchase CD's of relaxation techniques that have been professionally produced. You can typically find these in the audio book section of your local full service bookstore, shelved with the self-help books. Many of these are simply wonderful, and I find that I use them often to facilitate the relaxation process. I have made relaxation CD's and tapes for my clients over the years, and they all appreciate having an actual voice to focus on. Actively listening to a person giving specific instructions can really help, but not everyone likes having someone chattering in their ear. My advice would be to give the following guidelines a try on your own, perhaps listening to music with headphones. If, after a few days of trying, you find you simply cannot get into the right frame of mind, head on over to your local bookstore and look at their selection. If you have an MP3 device, most of the music web sites offer relaxation downloads as well.

For some basic guidelines, read the following suggestions to help you learn to relax, reverse the impact of stress on your body, and introduce a mental calm that will carry over for hours after you are done. Remember to find a time and place when you will not be disturbed, and where you can either sit, recline, or lie down in comfort. This procedure should take, at a minimum, 10 minutes, but ideally you would spend 30 minutes in a relaxed state.

Procedure

Close your eyes. Take five or six deep breaths, as described in the previous section. Begin to allow your mind to unwind.

Focus on releasing any stress, worry, or concerns of the day. Instead, think about creating peace and relaxation in your mind and body.

You may want to repeat to yourself any words or phrases to help you begin to relax. Examples might include, "I am peaceful," "I am relaxed," "My mind is quiet," or "My mind is serene." Use whatever words or phrases helps you start to let go of tension. Do use words that are positive, and geared towards the state you are trying to achieve, rather than describing what you *don't* want to happen. For example, avoid thinking phrases such as, "I am not stressed," "I don't want to feel overwhelmed," or "I don't want to think about my upcoming product party tonight." Just as having a vision for your life helps you achieve it, saying to yourself what you *want* to feel helps you achieve that way of being.

Then let your breathing return to normal, but relaxed and calm.

Now, move your focus from breathing and peaceful self talk to the muscles in your body. You will be concentrating on various parts of your body, starting from your head and working your way down to your feet. At each major muscle group, focus on only those muscles. Then you will contract and tighten the muscles, holding that contraction for about two or three seconds. It may seem contradictory to tense muscles when you ultimately want to relax them, but this method will help you re-educate your brain to know what your muscles should feel like when they are relaxed by juxtaposing it against them feeling tense.

When we spend so much time in a harried and rushed state, we actually forget what our muscles should feel like when they relax. It's almost a foreign feeling! By tensing them, then releasing the tension, we force the muscles to be in a non-tense state. Your muscles will naturally and quickly let go of the contraction and you will experience an immediate wave of relaxation across them. However, you should NEVER tense muscles to the point of pain. You will feel tension and it will feel as if it requires much energy to maintain the tension, but you should not feel pain.

You then concentrate on how much better your muscles feel when relaxed. In this way, you remind yourself what they should feel like. You can then be more aware of when they start to hold tension because of stress, and you can take measures to decrease the stress.

Start the process at your head. Think about the muscles in your scalp and forehead. Concentrate on them, feeling any tension that might be in those muscles. Next, contract or tighten those muscles in your scalp and forehead. Hold the tension for just two or three seconds, and then let go of the tension. Notice how quickly your muscles release the tension, how rapidly the muscles let go of the unpleasantness. And note how much better your muscles feel when you let them relax. Become aware of how smooth and loose they feel. If you need to tighten those muscles again in order to achieve the sense of release once more, repeat the procedure.

Once you have finished focusing on your forehead, move to the muscles around your eyes and your nose. Feel the tightness that might already be there. Then tense these muscles, scrunching up your eyes and nose to create tension and strain. Pay attention to how much energy it requires for your muscles to be tense. Then, after holding the tension for just a few seconds, let it all go. Feel how quickly the strain washes away, and how relieved and relaxed your eyes and nose feel.

Then move to the muscles in your neck and shoulders. Again, concentrate on this muscle group, noticing any tension that already exists there. Hunch up your shoulders and tighten your neck, taking care to avoid pain or over-tensing them. Hold just to the point of tension for a few seconds, then release and let go. It will feel as if a wave of relaxation has washed over them.

Continue this sequence of noticing existing tension in major muscle groups, tensing the muscles for a few moments, and then letting go of that tension. The contrast between how muscles feel when they are tense, versus when they are relaxed, should be very apparent.

Focus on the following major muscle groups: upper back, upper arms/biceps, stomach, buttocks, thighs, calves, and toes.

This technique is called *progressive muscle relaxation*, and it works particularly well for people who have never tried relaxation techniques before. Having a physical activity helps focus attention and gives you something concrete to think about. It teaches you to use muscle tension as a signal to you during the day for when your stress levels are elevated. So, you might find you are more sensitized to strain and pressure in your neck. When you feel that sensation, you can take a few moments to do some deep breathing and in about 30 seconds lower stress levels a bit.

Below, record your impressions of relaxation techniques. When will you try this for the first time? What time of day is best, and where in your house (or even your car!) will you do it? How will you make certain you will not be disturbed? And how much time each day will you devote to practicing relaxation?

_____

_____

_____
_____
_____
_____
_____
_____
_____
_____
_____
_____

Exercise

Here it comes – the lecture about the importance of exercise! Most likely you already have heard about the importance of exercise, not just for stress relief but for overall health and well being. And if you were not aware of the connection between regular exercise and good health, let me be quite clear – exercise enhances all areas of health, including mental, physical, emotional, and spiritual.

I do know about the difficulties in maintaining a consistent exercise program. Though I have exercised throughout most of my life, there have also been significant gaps of time when I didn't exercise. My primary excuse was that "I didn't feel like it." Profound, huh? And yet I think that is why many women don't work out regularly. It seems to take up so much effort and time, while we have a to-do list a mile long so we can build a thriving business and still take care of our families.

While the experts tell us we "only" have to exercise 30 minutes a day, most days a week, the reality is that exercise takes up more time than 30 minutes. For instance, let's assume you can exercise at home, either because you have some cardio equipment in the house, or because you go outside to walk or run. You have to change into your workout clothes, do some mild warm up and stretching, maybe locate your music player to keep you company along the way, and then get started with the actual 30 minutes of working out.

When you finish your cardio, you must then stretch in order to avoid muscle soreness and maintain or improve flexibility. You also have to cool down enough so that you still aren't sweating after you come out of the shower (this has happened to me, and it is supremely unpleasant). All of this adds perhaps 15 minutes onto your warm up and workout.

Then you hit the shower, followed by getting dressed and preparing yourself for the day. When it is all said and done, you have spent close to an hour getting ready to exercise, exercising, and then recovering from exercise, followed by half an hour showering and dressing. Of course, if you have to go to a gym for your workout, you need to add on the commute time back and forth to the facility, depositing your things in a locker, and then getting out onto the floor to exercise. Assuming you would normally shower and dress on a given day (and not everyone does that every single day!), the best case exercise scenario actually adds about an hour on to your day.

I would strongly argue that it is an *important and necessary* hour, but I also understand how time-strapped WAHMs see that hour as expendable. I will do my best to convince you that activity is important for many reasons. But the most compelling reason is that, if you exercise, you will feel better the entire day. You will get an almost immediate lift from activity, and the rest of your day will flow a bit more smoothly. Why? There are many physiologic reasons to explain this benefit, but the most relevant one is that exercise helps to burn off the residual build up in your body from the fight or flight response.

Remember all those changes your body goes through, all of them designed to help you perform some major physical activity? Because of our lifestyle, we don't actually do anything physical to cope with stress, forcing our body to store the waste products from the stress response. Exercise burns much of that stress by-product out of your system. In doing so, your body quite literally burns stress away.

Apart from this direct impact on relieving stress, exercise contributes to positive physical and emotional health in so many other ways. I will list some here, but realize this list is far from comprehensive, and the full extent of the positive impact of exercise is wide ranging.

- ✓ Exercise burns calories.
- ✓ The extra burned calories can keep body weight down.
- ✓ Lower body weight might enhance body image and how you feel about yourself.
- ✓ Lower body weight is healthier overall, with less chance of developing some chronic diseases such as diabetes.
- ✓ Exercise increases muscle mass in your body, causing you to burn more calories at rest than you would if you had less muscle mass.
- ✓ Weight bearing exercise builds bone density, making your skeletal system less susceptible to osteoporosis.
- ✓ Exercise actually makes you feel more energetic and better able to meet the demands of your life.
- ✓ Regular exercise lowers your resting heart rate and blood pressure, and can lower total cholesterol level.

I could go on, but I think you get the point. I know this information might not be enough to move some of you into action. And again, I understand. Sometimes it just seems like too much effort to plan an exercise, particularly if exercise is not something you enjoy.

So rather than assuming you will go right out and start a lifelong exercise program, simply because you read of its benefits here in this book, I will suggest another approach. If you do not currently exercise regularly, and you do not intend to start such a program in the near future, I'd like you to take a few moments to answer a few questions about exercise.

Since you are not going to exercise right now, list the reasons why.

_____
_____
_____
_____
_____

If you could have your ideal life that did include a regular exercise program, what would that program look like? What sorts of activities would you do? How often would you do them? Would you prefer to do really active, functional exercise like hiking, or do you envision yourself doing an aerobics class?

If circumstances were perfect for allowing you the time and space and motivation to exercise, what would those circumstances be?

When do you think those circumstances would be likely to happen?

I encourage you to re-visit this section many times in the future and ask yourself these same questions over and over. If nothing else, they might invite you to start thinking about the possibility of exercising at some point in the future. Or you might be inspired to start doing something right now, at whatever level you feel most comfortable with. For instance, there is no particular reason to start a jogging program. You could just commit to walking for one mile more than you normally do each day, perhaps taking your children with you to catch up on their day. Or you can use the time to walk the dog. Or you can use the time to dream and plan for what you will do the next day to move your business forward.

If you are interested in starting an exercise program, then consider the following questions:

What activity would I most like to do? Do I have the equipment I need, or access to the equipment? Are there any special requirements of this activity (i.e. is it a class at the gym that meets at set, regular times)?

_____
_____
_____
_____

What days are you best able to plan to work out? What time each day will you make available to exercise?

_____
_____
_____
_____

Is there an accountability system you can set up to make it more likely you will follow through consistently? Is there a friend who you could call regularly to "check in" with, keeping up accountability for you both? Could your husband/partner function as an accountability partner?

_____
_____
_____
_____

What is your current attitude towards exercise? Some people love it, but they simply allow other activities to take over their time. Some people really dislike exercise, particularly sweating. Some people like "real" activities, like skiing, hiking, road biking, tennis, basketball, or volleyball, and find structured exercises boring or pointless. Whatever your attitude, write down in the following space your relationship with exercise, including your attitude towards it.

_____
_____
_____
_____
_____
_____
_____
_____
_____

Although this book is not long enough to address all the common barriers people have to regular exercise, I will attempt to guide you through a process designed to help you along a path of more regular physical activity. Please recall the vast array of benefits exercise affords you. Even if stress relief does not top your list of reasons to move your body, know that every minute you engage in exercise is akin to putting money in the bank for the future – regular, appropriate activity builds the bodily equivalent of a savings account. Exercising now increases the likelihood of a healthier future.

You do not have to *like* exercise in order to *participate* in it. Certainly, picking an activity that you actually like to do will make it easier to stick with it. But if there truly is nothing you like to do, pick something you can live with. Walking is always a good choice for people like this. You can walk anywhere and everywhere, and you don't have to work up a sweat in order to benefit (although getting your heart rate up will give you more benefits). Just walk briskly and for at least 20 minutes most days of the week. If you wait until you "like" walking, you will never do it. Just start the plan because you know that by doing so, you are taking care of yourself.

Another technique that most people can use is to re-purpose exercise into something you DO enjoy. For instance, use your walking or exercise time as your time to go over the events of the day, organize and plan your next meeting, figure out what to have for dinner that night, and so on. In other words, turn your exercise time into planning time. If you are on an exercise bike, you can even keep a pad of paper beside you to jot down notes. In this way, you are accomplishing two important stress relief strategies at one time – planning and exercising.

But your exercise time doesn't have to only consist of planning time – you can use it to pray, meditate, or listen to the latest download of your favorite podcast or audiobook. By using your exercise time to accomplish these other tasks, you might find that you actually accomplish *more* than if you didn't exercise. Otherwise, when would you really take the time to listen to the latest best seller?

In my opinion, technology makes re-purposing exercise convenient and easy. Downloading podcasts and books, certainly, but there are also many web sites that offer workout downloads to MP3 players, with fitness instructors talking you through specific workouts and keeping you motivated and on-task. Of course, you can't go wrong with listening to great music, but if it still isn't your "thing," feeling as if you are getting something *other* than exercise done can be wonderful.

Keeping this re-purposing idea in mind, in the following space, record some things you could possibly do during your exercise time to feel more productive. Feel free to skip this section if exercise is something you already enjoy.

_____
_____
_____
_____
_____

_____

_____

If you generally enjoy exercising, but always find reasons *not* to do it regularly, you might also benefit from the suggestions I offered for those women who really do not like exercise. However, you may have other challenges, such as boredom, time management issues, or small children to attend to while exercising. Each of these scenarios presents unique issues. But the overriding theme for you will be to refer to your vision of how you want your life to be. Understand what you want to create in your life in terms of activity, and how you envision it fitting into your lifestyle. Returning your focus to the big picture of your life as a whole can help you find your motivation when it wanes (and it will wax and wane, be sure about that!).

If boredom is a problem for you, then you will need to attempt new and interesting activities. This may seem obvious, but you may not have gone to the next step of actually figuring out what that new and interesting activity will be. Guess what? Now's that time!

In the following space, record your history of exercise, meaning the types of activities you have done in the past, and what you liked and didn't like about each of them. Try to be as specific as possible about your pros and cons list, because having clues about the characteristics of activities you gravitate towards may pave the way towards finding new ones. It can shed light on the things you enjoy most.

_____
_____
_____
_____
_____
_____
_____
_____
_____

_____
_____
_____

Now, knowing what you historically have liked and disliked, it is time to brainstorm for new activities that might spark your interest. It is not necessary that you find the "perfect" exercise right now, but this will hopefully jump start your mind into considering alternatives. Try not to censor your brainstorming session – one of the big advantages of brainstorming is that we can be outrageous and even a bit unrealistic. Outlandish ideas always tap into a part of us that longs to try something different, and allowing that process to happen can initiate ideas in your head that may eventually materialize into something really fun for you. Jot down any ideas that sound like it might be fun to try, things that you would actually try if given a chance, like mountain climbing or swimming the English Channel or jogging a half marathon. Give free reign to your imagination!

_____
_____
_____
_____
_____
_____
_____
_____
_____
_____

My hope is that something on this list stimulates you to try a new activity that will help you overcome the boredom so often a problem with exercise programs. Approach your quest for a new interest in the same way you might approach anything else meaningful – with direct intention to find something great, with patience, and with determination. Inevitably, the right exercise will show itself to you, and will revitalize your exercise program.

If time management is your greatest obstacle, a few concerns must be addressed. First, if you actually lack the hours in the day to exercise, I would suggest getting up earlier in the morning to work out. Not everyone likes this option, but for many of us, it is the only way to have the time to do it. Also, research shows that people who plan to exercise in the mornings are more likely to stick to their exercise programs than those who exercise later in the day. Early morning work outs are not for everyone, but can present a reasonable option allowing us the time to care for ourselves.

Secondly, if rising earlier is not an option because you already get up very early, I would respectfully suggest reevaluating your schedule to determine what events and obligations you can eliminate to create the time you need to take this basic, critical step in self care. Perhaps you have stretched yourself thin enough that there is no room for error adjustment. If this is the case, how do you care for yourself? Are you doing other things to nurture your mind, body, and spirit to offset your jammed schedule?

Regular exercise is important enough for you to learn to say "no" to things that take up too much time. Regular exercise is important enough for you to drop activities that others can do, or that simply lack true value. Failing to take care of your body through exercise will eventually lead to a general breakdown and inability of your body to do the things you will want it to do. While it may seem like a huge barrier to find the time to exercise, remember that every bit of healthy activity banks a greater likelihood for a healthy, active future.

If you have the time to exercise, but have not grasped control over your schedule enough to corral those hours into a workout schedule, it might be time to change things. Again I encourage you to return to the vision of your life that you generated in Chapter 4. This is what you work for every day, towards which all of your efforts are oriented. If you want to include exercise into your life because you know the benefits it brings, the time has come to make it happen!

Now it simply becomes a matter of identifying what time you do have, when you will commit to exercising, and then making an appointment with yourself to do it. You may have heard the idea of "making an appointment with yourself for exercise," and not have taken it seriously. It sounds reasonable, but the reality may feel kind of silly, particularly if you haven't been exercising regularly recently.

I strongly suggest that you write down your intention to exercise. Put it directly on your "to-do" list if you keep one each day, and take one step farther by writing down the time of day and the exact activity you will do. As in many other areas, the more specific you are in writing down your intentions, the more apt you are to follow through with them.

The next area of difficulty is procrastination, distractions, or some combination of the two. When it comes time to work out, many things can get in the way, such as doing a load of laundry, checking email, sweeping the floor, or generally surfing the internet.

Here, record the things that act as distractions or that you tend to procrastinate with. Be brutally honest and be comprehensive. Greater accuracy will help you prevent derailment of your best exercise intentions.

_____
_____
_____
_____
_____
_____
_____

Awareness of your distractions is the first step towards tackling this common problem. The next step is to "catch yourself" when you start to gravitate towards those actions. For instance, if you set aside the time right after the bus picks up your children for school as your exercise time, you might find yourself tempted to check email first. Know this as a trigger for you, one of your red flag situations that will disrupt your plans.

The most effective technique in this circumstance, once you realize you are allowing yourself to be distracted, is to pay attention to your self-talk. Rat yourself out by telling yourself, in no uncertain terms, "I am allowing myself to be distracted, and I'm procrastinating." Once you say these words either out loud or in your mind, you then tell yourself that you WILL go for your workout, you WILL turn off the computer right now, and NOTHING will distract you from your goal.

You should never underestimate the power of self talk – it governs about 95% of our behavior every single day, so blunt honesty about what you are *really* doing will jar you out of the rationalizations we delude ourselves with all the time ("Oh, but I just need to check my emails for 15 minutes here, and then I'll go for my walk!") People are excellent at justifying whatever decision they make. It doesn't make the rationalization beneficial to you, but on the surface we feel justified in continuing our actions.

It will take effort, and it will take some adjustment to learn to talk honestly to yourself. But I can guarantee the energy you put into this work will pay off enormously when you find you can talk yourself into sticking with your exercise program.

If you have young children who cannot entertain themselves while you work out, you may have to institute more interventions in order to exercise regularly. If getting up early in the morning to work out before your children wake up will not work for you, another possibility is to work out while they nap. However, this might also be the time you have set aside to work on your business.

In this instance, you have a few options. One is to exercise both days of the weekend. Hopefully you have some sort of relief from child care over the weekends, either because a spouse can be "on-duty" or because you have family members who can watch your children while you take an hour each day to work out. While this is not an ideal way to spread out exercise over the course of a week, it might be your best option – and then right away you have exercised twice in that week.

Another great idea is to hire a mother's helper, typically a neighborhood girl or boy around age 12 or so who can come in and entertain your children for you while you exercise. You can feel more comfortable leaving the house for a two mile walk around the neighborhood, and your children will get to play the entire time. You can even bring a walkie-talkie with you to maintain constant contact. The potential problem with this arrangement is that you would be limited to when your mother's helper is out of school, unless you find a homeschooled pre-teen willing to take the job.

If you can't locate a reliable mother's helper, you can arrange for child care swap with another mom in your area. This would then of course mean that you would reciprocate by watching her children, but the built in accountability you would have with each other could be a bonus to the arrangement. Or certainly offering to pay someone to watch your children for an hour once or twice a week could also work for you.

As a mother of young children, having that hour to yourself a handful of times a week can serve many functions beyond simply improving your physical health. You will have those hours to focus entirely on yourself and whatever you want to think about. You can day dream, plan for dinner that night, think about a shopping list or your to-do list for the next day. Regardless of what else you use the time for, simply having a short break can work wonders for mental health.

For a fun twist, find ways to incorporate your children in your work outs. Jogging strollers are wonderful investments and allow you to interact with your children while getting some exercise. Plus, your children are watching you take good care of yourself, something they will file away in their memories and recall when they become adults. You are teaching them how to care for themselves as you care for yourself. Running around playgrounds and using the equipment for strength training is also fun – you can do push-ups on the ground, sit ups on the slide, chin ups on a bar, calf raises on train ties or short walls, and good old fashioned squats.

Hopefully this chapter convinced you of the importance of regular physical exercise, and how critical it is to incorporate it into your life. If you are physically fit, many other issues will be easier to handle. If I haven't convinced you to start an exercise program, my wish is that at a minimum you understand the impact of the choices you make by *not* working out, and that, as parents, we model those choices for our children. You don't need to be a body builder, or even to run three miles every day. Regular, consistent exercise will make a difference, and will lessen the impact of stress on your mind and your body.

Chapter 6 – Is Your Mind Your Worst Enemy?

Way back in Chapter 1, I introduced the definition of stress, being "the perception that the demands being made of us exceed your perceived ability to meet those demands, with the resources you have right now." I mentioned the importance of the word "perception" in that definition, and how we can change our perceptions of events in order to change our stress levels. In the last chapter, I mentioned the role of our self talk in helping us stick to an exercise program.

In this chapter, I will expand both of these ideas to help you learn to moderate the amount of stress that you feel. By changing your perception of the world, you will change the internal dialogue that goes on inside your mind, which leads to the experience of stress (or any other emotion for that matter, but for this workbook we will focus on stress). This may seem like a strange concept, but developing the ability to evaluate your perception of different events can have a profound impact on your life.

When I use the terms "internal dialogue" or "self talk," I am really using two different ways of saying the same thing – namely, the thoughts and beliefs that we have in our minds. Any time a thought crosses your head, an idea occurs to you, a long and firmly held belief flits into your awareness, you are experiencing internal dialogue, or self talk. Our thoughts and beliefs are critically important in how we approach the world, because the way we respond emotionally and behaviorally to any specific event is determined primarily by our thoughts.

What does this mean? It means that an event, in and of itself, does not "make" us feel stressed. It is the meaning we attribute to that event, it is the thought or belief we have about the event that precipitates the emotional response. Remember the example I gave back in Chapter 1 about driving on a busy highway? When we believed the driver was a true jerk, only out for himself and unconcerned with the safety and well-being of the other drivers, we felt angry and highly irritated. However, when we believed the driver to have a logical and reasonable cause for driving erratically, we felt only mildly irritated, and considerably less emotional.

During that example, the only thing that changed was the thoughts going through our heads *about* the way he was driving. If that event really happened, we would have no way of knowing the driver's true motivation of course (unless you happened to see this same exact driver every single day, and he repeatedly drove in an unsafe manner). If we ever encounter an event such as this, we have a choice about what to believe – we can believe that the driver is a jerk, or that the driver has a good reason for driving in that manner.

We could ask ourselves, "What evidence can I find that this person truly is a jerk?" Look for logical, rational evidence that this person drives in this way just because he can. If you cannot find such evidence, then you might ask yourself, "Could he have a good reason for driving that way? Does such a reason exist?" Would you want someone else judging your behavior when you are at your most stressed and overwhelmed? Extending mercy to others in the way we would want it extended to us not only makes logical sense, but it will make you feel better.

You may come to understand that there are probably dozens of possible reasons to justify erratic driving. And the possibility exists that this person has one of those reasons. We may not have evidence to prove it, though, just as we have no evidence to prove that he is a jerk.

So what to do then? Now it becomes a choice you can make. Do you choose to believe he is a jerk, and feel angry and irritable? Or do you chose to believe he has some reason for driving like that, and while we may never know what it is, we can feel better *right now* about the situation as a whole? That driver won't care which way you choose to feel, but I'll bet *you care!* It could mean the difference between arriving home in a rotten mood, and arriving home with a smile on your face.

You can see how our self talk directly impacts our emotions and stress level. While it may seem difficult to believe at first, this is really good news because we can learn to pay attention to our self talk and sometimes alter it if we want to get better control of our emotions. Often times, our internal dialogue consists of thoughts and beliefs that are skewed or even blatantly irrational. Yet, because we are so used to these thoughts in our heads, we don't ever stop to make sure they even make sense before acting on them. It would be like the CEO of a corporation having an idea to move the business in a new direction, then implementing that new course without gathering data, researching the market, and consulting with her executive team. Business people generally make decisions after discussing ideas out loud, so that different people can evaluate the logic and soundness of the concept.

In contrast, in our own lives, we make decisions all the time based only on our own belief system. Not only do we fail to ask someone else if that belief makes sense, but we don't even *ask ourselves* if it makes sense! We just have a thought and we go with it, in the absence of supporting evidence.

Of course, most of our actions during the day definitely do not require a meeting of an executive committee in order to execute them. But you can learn how to be your own "executive committee" when it comes to managing your stress level. As with most everything else, it will require some time and attention, but if you master these techniques, you will notice overall reductions in stress and anxiety.

The first step is to become conscious of the thoughts and beliefs you have about particular events or situations. This is a skill that may take a few days to really get the hang of, so be patient. Set an intention to become aware of the specific thoughts or beliefs that *go* through your mind.

The best way to start this habit is to notice when you experience a change in your emotional state. For instance, if you notice you start feeling frustrated about something during the day, stop yourself for one moment and reflect on the event or situation that triggered the frustration you feel. Try to be objective about the event, describing in your mind ONLY what happened, not how you feel about what happened and why you may or may not feel justified in feeling that way.

After going over the objective series of events in your mind, focus on the thoughts or beliefs you have about this situation. What is your attitude or evaluation of it? What does it mean to you? What do you believe the impact will possibly be?

Be very careful that you do not mistake *feelings* for *thoughts*. People have a tendency to confuse thoughts and emotions, which will make this exercise more difficult. Emotions are more obvious (especially the negative ones) and make themselves known because we actually feel emotions in our bodies (that's why we use the phrase "I feel..." for when we experience emotions – because we quite literally do feel emotional changes in our bodies). Thoughts, however, more subtly move across our minds. Thoughts also tend to move more quickly, while emotions can linger and dissipate slowly.

It might challenge you to tease out the difference, but understanding this distinction will assist your efforts to relieve stress by helping you to avoid feeling stressed in the first place. If you can isolate your thoughts, you can then start to evaluate them in terms of their logic and truth. You might soon discover that some of your thoughts create artificial stress in your life (you'll see how in a few paragraphs).

As always, writing things down will help you clarify your process, so in the space below, pick an event that happened to you recently (maybe in the past few weeks). Choose an event to which you responded with some high level of emotion, but try not to choose an event or situation that touches on deeply ingrained emotional issues for you (such as chronic arguments with a sibling or conflicts with a parent). Pick a relatively benign event. Write out just the order of events here, not your reaction or thoughts about it, simply the "newspaper" version of what happened. For instance, you might write, "Suzie came home from school today telling me that I have to make 6 dozen cookies by tomorrow for the PTA bake sale because someone else's mom had to back out at the last minute. Suzie told her teacher that I would do it for the group."

_____
_____
_____
_____
_____
_____
_____
_____

Next, try to identify the thoughts or beliefs that went through your mind as you witnessed or experienced the event. Concentrate only on your thoughts, not your emotional reactions. You might write something such as, "I know I don't have time to bake the cookies by tomorrow, and everyone will be mad at me if I don't do it." Or, "Suzie's teacher won't think kindly of me if I don't do this, and I could ruin the PTA's attempt to raise money for their project."

_____
_____
_____
_____
_____
_____
_____
_____

Having isolated your thoughts about this event, it is now time to record your emotional reaction to this event. Continuing with our bake sale example, you might write, "I felt panicked, guilty, irritated, put upon, and generally stressed out."

_____
_____
_____
_____
_____
_____

Lastly, record any behavioral consequences you noticed as a result of feeling this way. You may or may not have actually done anything in response, but if you did, write about it here. For example, "I did all six dozen cookies and didn't sleep that night at all. As a result, I woke up grumpy and yelled at the dog the next morning."

_____
_____
_____
_____
_____
_____

Now it is time to evaluate those thoughts and beliefs. I will provide some guidelines here, but do know that the overriding principle for assessing your thoughts is to look at how accurate they are. If you recall, we respond emotionally, and then often behaviorally, to our thoughts. If our thoughts are inaccurate, illogical, or irrational, our emotional and behavioral reactions will also be illogical and out of proportion to the event.

The Tendency to Catastrophize

Sometimes we have thoughts that reflect an overreaction to an event, or what *could possibly occur* as a result of something happening. This is referred to as "catastrophizing," or responding to something as if it were a catastrophe. This might be reflected in internal dialogue sounding like, "This is the most horrible thing that could happen, this is terrible and messes up the whole week, I'll never get where I want to be, this is the worst thing that could happen!"

Are you a "worry-wart?" When you hear about something, is your first reaction along the lines of, "I wonder what could go wrong?" Or, "What if that happens to me?"

Anyone who truly believed that an event is "the most horrible thing that could happen" would be justified in feeling stressed, angry, sad, or any number of highly unpleasant emotions. Certainly thinking that a tragedy will possibly happen to you would also reasonably create stressful, fearful feelings. Those emotions make logical sense when confronted with something you believe to be truly horrendous.

However, we need to step back and evaluate our thoughts to make sure they are rational. Why feel needlessly stressed?

The best technique to counteract a tendency to catastrophize is to rank the event or situation on a scale from 1 to 10 in terms of how bad the event objectively is. On this scale, a jet plane crash that kills everyone on board would warrant a "10" ranking, while a hang nail or stubbing your toe would rank a "1." With this to guide our perspective, we can take any situation and understand how bad it "truly" is relative to other events. We can then modify our emotional response to reflect the true severity of the circumstance.

Sometimes we react to something as if it is a "7" when in reality it is a "2." Knowing this, we can take a moment to objectively evaluate our appraisal of the situation. Then, we can react with a more appropriate level of emotion or stress.

In the following space, record on a scale of 1 to 10 how severe the situation you described previously was.

_____
_____

Now, record on a scale of 1- 10 how strong your emotional reaction was to that event when it happened. In retrospect, did you overreact?

In the case of anticipating the worst case scenario, asking yourself to rate the true likelihood of it happening can alleviate some worry. As parents, hearing about child abductions and child abuse on the news can trigger anticipatory fear – "What if something happens to *my* child?" Watching the news strikes panic in the hearts of all parents when we allow ourselves to contemplate the possibility of ever having to face such a true tragedy.

Anxiety and stress happen easily when we worry about events that haven't happened. Sometimes we make another self talk error by believing that we can somehow plan for truly catastrophic events, or that we can inoculate ourselves against the emotional impact of a theoretical disaster. In the case of possible child abduction or exploitation, there is no way to "prepare" for that happening, no way of vaccinating ourselves against the enormous pain and hurt it would bring.

Therefore, it often makes most sense to tell ourselves NOT to think about those events. Statistically they are highly unlikely to occur. Also tell yourself that if, God forbid, something like that did happen, you would do whatever was needed in order to get through it. You would figure it out at that time and move forward. Worrying about it will not prevent it from happening, nor will it prepare you in any way for dealing with it. There is no way to truly emotionally prepare for a catastrophe. Let it go.

The Nasty Words: "Should" and "Must"

The next area in which people tend to make errors in internal dialogue is in word choice. Specifically, we tend to create stress in our lives by telling ourselves that we "should" do something, or we "must" or "ought to" accomplish that thing. How many times a day do we pass these words by our lips out loud? And how many more times a day do these words pass through our brains?

You may wonder, "What's the big deal about knowing that you *should* do something? Maybe you REALLY should do it!"

I will suggest to you that, in life, there really are very few "shoulds" or "musts." Indeed a couple of them exist – you *should* clothe your children, you *should* love them, you *must* feed them, you *ought to* feed yourself. You *should not* kill or harm someone else. You *should* stop at stop lights and stop signs.

The words "should" and "must" imply a moral imperative. In other words, something truly horrible will happen if you fail to do something you "should" do, or if you violate something you "ought not to do." Imagine the consequences if you did not stop at a stop light, or if you didn't feed your children. These could result in real catastrophes.

The fact is that "should" and "must" have become such an ingrained part of our external and internal vocabulary. We use these words all the time, without real thought as to their impact on our lives. If overall you lead a low stress life, then perhaps examining your use of these words is not needed. However, for many of you, it might be time to pay attention to just how many times we tell ourselves we (or someone else) "should" do something.

The harm comes because often times it simply *is not true* that we "should" do that task. It is likely that our lives might be easier, better, more fulfilled, or in some way improved if we do the task. But we might not actually have to do it for fear of something horrible happening.

When we speak to and about ourselves (and others) regarding a chore or errand, consider using more accurate, less morally imperative language. Instead of saying to yourself, "I must make those cookies or the PTA won't raise enough money," say to yourself, "If I make the time to bake the cookies, the PTA might raise more money and I might feel better about contributing in this way."

Rather than saying, "I must make these cookies or the PTA and the teachers won't like me," say, "I can make these cookies if I choose to, and it would be in the PTA's best interest for me to help them in this way."

Can you notice the difference in the emotional reactions you might experience by removing the idea of the task as something that "needs" to be done? By shifting your thought process to one of less pressing need, you deflate your stress reaction and adopt a more problem-solving, altruistic attitude (because you understand that you are doing the PTA a favor, and that the future health and well being of the organization does not in fact rest on your shoulders). You may still be displeased at the idea of staying up all night making cookies, but perhaps you feel less stressed about doing it.

What areas in your life do you tend to approach with "shoulds" when you could replace them with "it would be in my best interest if….," or, "it might be nice if….," or "I'd like it if…..?" Take a day to pay attention to how often you say those words to yourself – you'll probably be quite surprised! Record a few of those self talk statements here:

_____
_____
_____
_____
_____
_____
_____
_____

Next, rewrite those statements, replacing the words "should" or "have to" or "must" or "ought to" with more accurate self talk, such as "it would be better if," or "this might make things easier later on if I…." or "it is in my best interest to…"

_____
_____
_____
_____
_____
_____
_____
_____

Do you notice any difference in how you might experience the situations differently by changing your internal dialogue? Isn't it nicer and less stressful to know that you participate in activities not because you "must," but because it is in your best interest? Or that you choose to engage in events because you want to make life a bit easier for someone else, not because you "have to?"

You are taking control of your life by ridding your brain of the nasty "shoulds." By rewording the reasons for your deeds, you shift from a place of high anxiety driving your decision making to a place of sound rationale. You aren't baking the cookies under duress, but instead because you *choose* to make them for a specific purpose that benefits someone else.

No More All-or-Nothing Thinking!

Another way our internal dialogue can derail us is engaging in "all-or-nothing" thinking. This means believing that a situation must be all one way, or it can be nothing. So many examples of this occur every day – are there any that come to mind right away?

As a business owner, it can be easy to fall into this negative thought pattern. You may have exciting ideas about building your business, and ambitious goals to meet for finding new clients each month, or increasing your revenue for a week.

Sometimes when a goal is set and we don't meet it, it might be easy to think, "Well, I didn't meet my new client goal this month, so I must not be good at recruiting new clients. Maybe I should give up." This is akin to saying, "If I can't be perfect, I am a failure." This is simply untrue! Many things could have accounted for not meeting your goal in one particular month, starting with the possibility that your goal was unrealistic to begin with. If you wanted to increase your client base by 5, and you increased it by 2, I see lots of reasons to celebrate, not despair.

To manage stress, try to step back and be realistic and understand that sometimes reaching goals comes in phases. Parents make this error (albeit unwittingly and with a kind heart) with their children. Has your child ever come home from school with a grade less than an "A?" If your child comes home with a "B," is your first thought or comment, "Why didn't you get an A?" This is all-or-nothing thinking – the only acceptable outcome is an "A" and anything less is essentially failure. Focusing on only on what the grade *isn't* negates all the child *has* learned.

Perhaps the child in fact needs to learn better study or test taking skills, but sending the message that decent passing grades are less than acceptable demonstrates how all-or-nothing thinking devalues success. Of course it is great to strive for the highest grade possible, but sometimes a child simply will not score as high as other children. Assuming the child put forth adequate effort, sometimes a "B" or "C" is good enough.

Perfectionism (all-or-nothing thinking) is a stress, setting up imaginary rules for yourself and others. It closely relates to the "should" problem – "things should be a particular way, or I can't be happy/satisfied/successful." Sometimes the network and multilevel marketing businesses inadvertently feed this irrational thought pattern. Many clients have told me about how energized and motivated they feel following their company's yearly convention. They return home with great ideas and inspiration to sell new product lines and improve the lives of the customers they serve.

They also return home with a vision in their heads of how their lives might be if they worked harder. As an effective way of motivating their independent consultants, these companies will showcase the most financially successful consultants in the business. Often times they are women, and these women tell their stories of reaching financial freedom and leading the lifestyle they could have only dreamt of years before. They are living proof that certain techniques and approaches work to create sustainable business lines.

I applaud these women for achieving such fabulous success, and it is admirable that they pass along their ideas and motivation. It provides a vision for the other consultants to aspire to, a concrete path towards success.

The potential pitfall comes when the consultants return home with this vision, and six months later have not progressed as rapidly as they had hoped. In this instance, someone with a perfectionist or all-or-nothing thought pattern might say to themselves, "I didn't make it to where that woman was, so I'm probably not cut out for this business."

To curtail this tendency, I urge you to return to your vision for your life that you fashioned back in Chapter 3. Read it two or three times. *That* is your goal, *not* the woman at your convention! It is hard to resist the temptation to absorb someone else's goal as our own, particularly when that person's goal appears compelling and highly attractive. However, it is still *not your goal!* Those women are different from you, they have different backgrounds and husbands and values and goals than you have. They may have had to work 60 hours a week for a year or more to attain that level of accomplishment – are you willing to make a similar commitment?

If so, then wonderful! And if not, that's wonderful, too! Your business needs to work for YOU! If making $750 per month consistently allows you to live a satisfying lifestyle, then by all means, be content. You may have other business owners around you talking about growth and expansion. You might feel pulled into such a heady conversation. But if the effort required to reach that endpoint does not fit into your vision, again ground yourself in the balance of your life. Your future may present more time and energy for you to grow your business, but if it works for you now the way it is, then what more could you realistically ask for?

Comparing yourself with uber-successful WAHM's will generate needless stress. Be honest with what you want and how much time you have for your business. Then commit to that time, releasing any self talk saying "I'm not good enough because I'm not working hard enough." Honor what makes you feel most fulfilled, knowing you simply cannot commit full time hours to every important thing in your life (and still feel good about your life).

Take a few moments and honestly record below the names or initials of the women you tend to compare yourself to:

_____

_____

Reflecting on the list above, consider what it would be like to let go of the need to compare. Answer the following question:

What would it be like if I no longer looked at other women and judged my current situation based on how it appears *they* handle their lives?

My guess is that many of you will realize the liberation and freedom you feel when you do not sit in judgment of yourself. Comparing your life with that of another person creates an artificial stress. You simply do not know what goes on behind closed doors, and if you did, I can just about guarantee you would no longer wish yourself in that person's shoes. Over the course of my career, I have seen many "perfect women who have it all" suffer from anxiety and depression, have verbally abusive husbands, are secret shoplifters, and feel a profound sense of not deserving all the outward blessings they have.

Plus, comparing yourself to someone else means you define your own personal satisfaction using someone else's measuring stick. Stay with your own fantasy of how you want your life to look and how you want to feel. Resist the urge to put others on a pedestal. Allow your internal dialogue to be supportive and realistic about your desired life.

Banishing Inappropriate Guilt

While it may be a condition of motherhood, I believe inappropriate guilt is something we can at least minimize and contain. Reducing guilt will have an enormous impact on your stress level, and can also result in more energy and motivation. I often wonder if women actually have a genetic predisposition to feeling guilty, as it seems on the surface as if men aren't plagued by the same albatross!

Whether our DNA causes our guilt or not, women seem to deal with it all the time. Women appear to have expertise in figuring out how participation in some activity will detract from someone else's life. Therefore, we shouldn't do something because....gasp!...we might be selfish! If we say "no" to the PTA's request for cookies because we need sleep that night, we feel guilty. If we have a chance to book three product parties in one weekend, we feel guilty because our spouses will have to entertain the children for a long time. If we want to exercise, we feel guilty because we haven't spent enough time with our neighbors this season. If we want to just sit and watch television, we feel guilty because the house is a mess and the dishes are still in the sink, and the lawn needs to be mowed and....well, you get the idea.

Guilt stinks. If you have a vision for your life that prioritizes time with your children and family, and you have developed a workable schedule to meet everyone's basic needs, there is no room for guilt. Feeling guilty is a direct result of more faulty internal dialogue. It likely resembles this statement, "Someone else might need me, and I can deal with situations better because I know all the ins and outs of what is going on. If I am away for a long time, something might not get done, or worse, might get messed up. Therefore, I need to put other things on hold so that I can be available." Or, you might believe, "My desires and wishes aren't as important as others' are, so if I indulge myself, I'm being selfish – so I feel guilty."

Patently untrue, all of it! It is now time to acquire a realistic, logical place for guilt in our lives. And it all starts with the dictionary.

Here is how Merriam-Webster defines the word "guilt:"

The fact of having committed a breach of conduct, especially violating the law and involving a penalty; the state of one who has committed an offense especially consciously.

In the following space, please write down how your lifestyle choices, or some situation or event you want to do, meet the criteria for feeling guilty. In other words, guilt is an appropriate response when we have committed some crime, or we have neglected a true "should or must" in life. In what specific way does it make sense for you to feel guilty?

_____
_____
_____
_____

It is my sincere hope that you have written NOTHING in the above space! Unless you are ignoring your children on a regular basis, neglecting their basic care, and totally disregarding your spouse or partner, then guilt is an inappropriate emotion. Beyond being inappropriate, it consumes so much energy, time and attention that could be placed elsewhere. If anything, guilt pulls you away from life, rather than motivating you towards fulfilling perceived commitments. When we act out of guilt, we eventually end up feeling resentment. Resentment festers and morphs into irritation and anger.

The advantage to ridding one's self of guilt is enormous. Guilt serves to pull people out of whatever they are experiencing. It is a barrier to full engagement living. When we feel guilty, we are not living in the present moment, and the moment is then gone. This repeats itself over and over again – before you know it, life is passing by and you aren't even living it. You are spending it feeling guilty, rather than actually spending time doing the things you feel guilty that you aren't doing!

The Problem of Multitasking

If I could wish one thing for each of you, it would be to cut multitasking by 80% in your life. I first began paying attention to the impact of multitasking a few years ago when clients started to call in to our sessions from their cell phones while they were also doing other things (sometimes shopping, sometimes going to the UPS store, sometimes going through the drive through of a fast food place). I began to wonder how much of our conversation they were able to absorb while dividing their attention in such a manner.

Recently I started a policy asking clients to "protect" their coaching sessions by only concentrating on our discussion. But this experience led me to the realization of how disengaged people are becoming. Unfortunately, multitasking has become a way of life for many, aided by cell phones, wireless internet, and personal digital assistants. Although research has shown that women tend to be superior to men in our ability to multitask, I think we have taken things a bit too far….

You might be thinking, "I have to multitask in order to accomplish all the things on my to-do list – it's what keeps me effective and efficient at getting everything done. How can I give it up?"

You can reduce your reliance on multitasking, while maintaining the WAHM lifestyle. It might possibly involve paring down your commitments, saying "No" to things that you simply do not have the time for. You may wonder why you should even consider doing that, since you are able to accomplish so much more while multitasking – it doesn't make sense to try to do *less,* does it?

Yep, it does make a lot of sense. Here's why – multitasking is an illusion. It gives the impression that someone completes so many things. In actuality, the multitasker has only been marginally involved in any one activity, therefore meeting only minimal results.

Why? When we multitask, we spread our attention across many things at one time. This means that no one thing gets one hundred percent of our focus. We are not truly engaged or involved in any one activity – we only skim the surface of it just so we can cross it off a list. We haven't actually *done* it because we weren't really paying attention to it.

We reach the end of our day, and we may find that we crossed many things off a list. But where did the day really go? Were we even paying attention, in the moment, engaged and involved with anything meaningful? Or was the whole day un-lived? Sometimes we might have to have a day like this. The trouble comes when we rely on multitasking just to get through the day.

Mono-tasking (doing only one thing at a time) makes our worlds bigger – we have a more textured life, deeper connections, more meaningful moments and relationships. We are really living because we are paying attention to what is going on around us. Just as importantly, the people with whom we have connections will also experience this deeper engagement. From your children's perspective, they will know you are actually there with them. They will be more fully satisfied with the time you spend with them because you are filling them up with connections and a sense that they are important enough for you NOT to waste that time thinking about something else. What a gift!

To what extent do you rely on multitasking? Do you reach the end of your day and feel disconnected, but accomplished? Is this the way you wish to feel?

_____
_____
_____
_____
_____
_____
_____
_____

What would it be like for you to pay full attention to everything you do in one given day? How would that change your day and your perception of "accomplishment?"

_____
_____
_____
_____
_____
_____
_____
_____

This is simply food for thought, as I understand multitasking has become a way of life for so many people. However, I do challenge you to at least consider how your interactions with others might change and improve if you chose to be more present. It would be a matter of switching from a "quantity" perspective to a "quality" perspective in your life.

Chapter 7 - My Husband Doesn't Take My Business Seriously

One of the most frequent complaints I hear from clients and friends who run home based businesses is, "My husband doesn't think my business is serious and real. He rolls his eyes and doesn't support me." Has this happened to you?

I believe there are a few reasons that spouses and partners tend to minimize the legitimacy of the WAHM business. First, most WAHMs work part time hours. For some reason, part time work is generally viewed as less important and less impactful than full time work, even when the worker leaves the home to go to a job. The mentality behind this belief sounds something like, "If it isn't important enough to do full time, then it probably ISN'T important." Sounds like all-or-nothing thinking to me! But it does seem to represent a societal judgment. Can you imagine a man talking about his part time job? What kind of an impact would that make? How would he be perceived? Probably in a similar way as WAHMs are perceived.

But there is an important difference between WAHMs and "conventional" part time jobs – we do our jobs from the home. Why does this matter? Think of the connotations of the word "home." Generally it conjures images of coziness, eating, resting, and retreat. The vast majority of workers go home to get away from work, so the image of home is one of "anti-business." How can anyone accomplish anything business-related from the home?

A third consideration is the nature of the businesses towards which WAHMs gravitate. Many of them target female customers, such as skin care, home furnishings or accessories, jewelry, and clothing. Not only do the products appeal primarily to women, but they are many times sold in home parties. Although women have figured out how to sell to other women leveraging something we all like to do – gather together to socialize – from a male perspective, it might "just" look like a party. How can business be conducted in a party atmosphere?

Lastly, related to the part time hours most WAHMs work, most tend to bring in relatively lower salaries than their spouses and partners. Because of the amount of money involved, it might be seen as more of a hobby rather than an entrepreneurial venture. Because you "only" bring in a small amount of money (right now, at least!), others might underestimate the power of the lifestyle and business opportunity. How many times have you heard the business reporters talk about WAHMs on television? Or how many articles have you read in the newspaper or financial magazines about the economic clout of WAHMs? Remember, network marketing businesses alone bring in $32 billion each year – why isn't anyone talking about this?

All of these factors combine to create a situation ripe for misunderstanding and lack of support. When your spouse fails to take you and your business seriously, it feels like a major obstacle to overcome. It might be hard to plan parties or client calls if you worry about how your spouse will react to your use of time (this is where banishing the guilt exercise comes in handy!). And you might hold back investing financially in some part of your business because of how your spouse or partner might perceive the expense. The lack of support is often a "make or break" factor in the success of a home based business, so it is worthwhile to confront and address.

It Starts With You

In coping with an unsupportive spouse, many of the societal issues discussed previously might require a long time to overcome. I say this to help you develop realistic expectations for how far along, and how quickly, your spouse might come to understand the importance of your business. Some of the preconceived notions may take a while to overturn. Have faith, don't give up, and know that you are not alone!

But the very first thing you can do to help your husband view you as an entrepreneur is for you to see *yourself* as one, first. Think of this being an "inside-out" process. You *must* see yourself as a business person before anyone else will see you as such. Think about brick and mortar businesses, like the big box discount department stores or the big home improvement stores. They don't sit around and wait until someone starts buying from them before they go out and promote themselves as a business. They advertise themselves constantly as a business that can meet your needs as their customer, and come see them to shop!

Take this model and apply it to your business. To what degree do you currently view yourself as an entrepreneur/business person?

_____
_____
_____

Can you spend the next few minutes envisioning yourself as a true business person (because you ARE one)? What does it feel like? How does it feel differently from the way you feel now? How would you present yourself differently to your husband if you "owned" your sense of being an entrepreneur?

_____
_____
_____
_____
_____
_____
_____

If you have never run a business before, starting a home based business can be intimidating, and it is completely understandable if you have challenges developing your business-person identity. You may need reassurance from the important people around you, most notably any mentors you might have and your husband. If these people show any skepticism about your ability to succeed, you will probably internalize their reluctance and begin to doubt yourself even more. Having their support and encouragement will make everything easier.

However, an important note about your career identity – it must come from within you, not from an external source. This means that you cannot wait until others see you as an entrepreneur before you start to see yourself as one. They will be looking to you for signs of how you will conduct yourself and sell your product or service. As the leader of your business, it is up to you to set the tone of your company. You are the face of it, the tangible evidence of your venture. Others around you will not know how to interact with you as a business person until you establish the atmosphere you want to design.

Imagine if your image as an entrepreneur depended on someone projecting their idea of a business person onto you! You wouldn't have any control over how you are perceived and how you interact with customers. Quite quickly you would lose control over things, and it would all unravel.

So, stand firm in your role. Define it for those around you. If your husband doesn't treat you as a legitimate business owner, ask yourself if you behave tentatively around him about the company. Are you inclined to subtly ask his permission before scheduling business meetings or parties? For instance, might you approach him with, "Honey, I was thinking of meeting with a web site designer on Thursday night. Could you possibly watch the kids?" If he already minimizes your business, asking "permission" in this manner reinforces the idea that it isn't valid. If your husband had a business meeting one night, does he ask if you can watch the children that night before he schedules it?

If your business were bringing in $15,000 per month, would you be more forceful about stating your needs? If so, then you might consider being more forceful now. As long as you enjoy this work and it fits into your vision, it doesn't really matter how much money you are bringing in – if you have a need, you can state it in a way that sends the message of "This work is just as important to me as anyone else's work is to them."

With this new perspective, your question to your husband might be more bold: "Honey, I scheduled a meeting with a web site designer for Thursday night. Will you be home for the kids, or will you have to find a babysitter?" Admittedly, this is a more brazen statement and might not be one you feel comfortable using right now. But I strongly encourage you to at least start thinking this way in your mind.

The more your internal dialogue reflects your image as a business person, the more you will project that outward to everyone around you. See yourself talking about your business confidently, with enthusiasm, and with excitement. Envisioning yourself speaking like this, can you see how it might make a difference in how others perceive you? Feeling like an entrepreneur leads to talking like an entrepreneur. You will find yourself chatting about your company as an actual business, not just something you do "on the side."

In what ways can you better project yourself as a business person that you are not currently doing?

_____
_____
_____
_____
_____
_____
_____
_____
_____

More Significant Spousal Concerns

Certainly projecting your business person's attitude will help your husband, and others, know that you take this seriously. However, it might not completely change his mind and his level of support and encouragement. Sometimes there are fundamental marital issues that influence his attitude and opinion. In this case, I will emphatically encourage you to consult with a licensed mental health professional for couples' counseling. If there are chronic, troublesome, or severe problems, trying to change his mind about your business is probably a futile effort. Please do reach out for help. The tips and techniques in this workbook are intended for generally stable, healthy, and loving relationships. They will not work in relationships that are in crisis. They will also not work in relationships based on competition and manipulation. If this characterizes your relationship, I urge to you consult with a qualified therapist to resolve these issues.

Even in a healthy, non-manipulative relationship, simply taking an inside-out approach will not be enough, and you will ideally want more support.

At some point, if you have not already done so, you and your husband would benefit from an honest, open conversation about your business. Occasionally, a husband has no input into the wife's decision to start a business – she just comes home from a product party as a new consultant. She is excited and optimistic, while he is stunned and confused, but happy to see her zeal.

Other times, a WAHM may have spoken to her husband about her venture, but after she starts it, challenges arise and she changes tactics and approaches. She may or may not share these changes with the husband, but eventually he sees how it might impact him, in terms of taking over child care, or making meals, or even financially from the checking account.

So if you feel an overall lack of support from your husband, plan a time for the two of you to discuss your business, both from your point of view, and from his point of view. In your fervor for your project, you may not have noticed how it affects your husband. Listen to what he has to say about it. He may feel pushed aside, as if you are putting in all of your time into this exciting endeavor, and he is sitting on the sidelines watching it all happen.

Is he feeling left out?

If so, this is extremely common for husbands of WAHMs. Sometimes for years, the husband's job has been the focus of all the attention and conversation. New experiences for you mean upheaval and change for people who haven't asked for it (including your children). This DOES NOT MEAN you should feel sorry for your husband, nor should you scale back on your excitement and gusto. But part of balancing this WAH lifestyle includes attending to your marriage. And important change for one member of a couple means change for the other member. Be mindful that those whom you love might feel neglected.

This is not to induce guilt (see previous chapter on how to avoid guilt)! It is a reminder, however, that the WAH lifestyle is in fact a lifestyle change for the entire family. I suggest refraining from an urge to condemn the feelings in your husband and others. Also, try to avoid competing with their feelings. For example, you might feel compelled to spout out, "How do you think I felt last year when you started your new job and were so excited by it, traveling all over the place while I stayed here at home?" The unsaid part of that comment might resemble, "Now it's your turn to feel left out," Although you might truly feel that way, saying it out loud is neither loving nor supportive, two characteristics you are trying to *increase* in your household.

One way to cope with this scenario of your husband feeling left out is to include him in your plans, your hopes, and your challenges. Open dialogue with him can help him feel included and more of a partner in your excitement.

Another tactic is to ask him what you could do so that he feels less neglected. It might be that there is nothing you can or should do, but sometimes just asking the question lets someone know that you care enough to consider doing something differently. It communicates to him your willingness to integrate his thoughts and feelings into your attempts to balance everything. The flip side of this possibility of course is that he does make a direct request of you. In that instance, you can consider whether you would be willing to meet the request. If not, be open to negotiating some middle ground, so that both of your needs are met.

Be open to the possibility that your husband might be concerned about you emotionally. If he works in the business world, he may be all too familiar with the obstacles you will face, and he might be scared to watch you struggle. Knowing you will face inevitable rejection as a business owner could trigger a protective mechanism in him, particularly if he knows you might take the rejection personally.

Again, open and honest communication is critical here. But so is his valuable work experience. If he knows the ins and outs of business, you might consider asking him for his advice on specific issues. During the course of your conversation, you might explain to him that you know this process will require personal growth and change for you. Sometimes you will operate out of your comfort zone, but you recognize the possibility and will tackle it as it comes.

On a more practical level, your husband might have financial concerns with a business start up. Particularly in the beginning, more money leaves the account than comes in for a while. Because money is such a hot button topic, it deserves a conversation all its own. Convey a willingness to alleviate his worry by negotiating a balanced approach to financing the venture. As a part of this conversation, make sure that your husband appreciates the emotional lift this business provides for you. Although you can't put a price on that, it might help him be more amenable to riding out the tough first few months. Have as a goal that by the end of your meeting together, you will have a money plan that makes you both feel sound and secure as you trot out your business.

On another level, your husband might feel threatened by the thought of your success. He might have certain ideas about who brings in the money in the household, and the idea of you working challenges deeply held beliefs. This is a tough one to deal with, because it underlines more significant marital role beliefs. Moreover, it cuts to the heart of his identity, and while a wife shouldn't have to sacrifice her own identity to preserve her husband's, changing his will take time and effort. Attempting to re-negotiate your role as a wife and mother in the middle of a marriage when things have been one way for so long will be difficult. In this case, a few sessions with a marital counselor who can help mediate this conversation might help. You might want to focus your approach on the aspects of your job that provide you meaning and esteem – namely, making a difference in others' lives, or meeting new people, or simply having something of your own.

Lastly, your husband might feel jealous of your new ideas and the potential in front of you. This feeling might be amplified if he is unhappy in his current position. Watching someone speak so enthusiastically about their career when you spend your days feeling underappreciated, unchallenged, underutilized, or just plain bored is really hard! Again, open lines of frequent communication can help manage these issues.

It ultimately comes down to the importance of connecting honestly and often with your husband. Express a genuine desire to understand his true concerns, and then make concerted efforts to address them and move forward. Hopefully this will result in a more supportive husband!

I suspect some of you might be thinking, "Why should I have this negotiation with my husband about all of this? If he were starting a new job, he wouldn't come to me asking me about MY concerns!" Indeed this might be true. But you are not your husband, and you get to do things the mature way, resolving conflicts and confusion via discussion and deliberation. Even if your husband would do things differently, if you want a different outcome, be willing to try different approaches.

Chapter 8 – Getting Control of Your Time

One of the great advantages of the WAHM lifestyle is the flexibility in scheduling business-related activities. One of the great DISadvantages of the WAHM lifestyle is the flexibility in scheduling business-related activities. What accounts for this paradox?

Most mothers start a home-based business with the idea that they will run their business around their household schedule. In fact, the ability to do this makes the WAH situation far more attractive than becoming an employee of a company that will require certain hours each week during specific times of the day. As WAHMs, however, we can pretty much work whenever we want.

Problems soon arise when you start to notice a tendency to check emails 30 times a day, and return phone calls when your children are trying to complete homework that also needs your attention, and you go over your paperwork for tax time at 11:00 at night, after the children and your husband fall asleep. Then when that paperwork is done, you check your email one more time because you're right there in front of your computer after all. Why not? By the time you are done, you look up at the clock and, lo and behold, it's 1:00 AM!

After a shortened night's sleep, you try to function the next day. In between loads of laundry and scrubbing toilets, you jam in bits of time here and there, planning for your next networking meeting and returning phone calls inquiring about your services. Before you know it, your children are home, and you check emails a few more times before running out of the house for sports practices. By the end of the day, your head hits the pillow just as you realize you forgot to print out the brochures you need for your meeting the next day. When would you have had time to do that today, anyway?

Attempting to run a business in between your normal activities makes most WAHMs feel crazed. While they may accomplish quite a bit, and might even have reduced multitasking as much as possible, they might still feel out of control with their schedule.

One of the first tasks I highly recommend to my clients is to establish regular business hours. All businesses have hours of operation, during which they serve their customers and conduct the nuts and bolts of moving a company forward. This is a powerful model to follow, and taking the time to organize your schedule to have specific business hours will help you streamline your organization and reduce your stress levels.

The first step in this process goes back to Chapter 4, in which you wrote down the activities you engaged in during a typical week. Looking at this schedule, you can see exactly how much time is required on a weekly basis for you to feel more in control of your work. Perhaps you added up a total of 12 hours of "work" time, not including all the stolen minutes checking emails and voice mails. Whatever your total, record that number of hours here:

_____

Now, look at the time you have available to devote to your business each week. When does this time fall during the week? Is it during school hours? Is it primarily on the weekend days? Or do they fall during the evening hours? Look for chunks of time, blocks of a few hours that you can segregate out of the rest of your non-business duties. Write down your available chunks of time here:

_____
_____
_____
_____
_____

Next, determine which of those chunks of time you will use for your business. It might be all of them, or just one or two of them. Your guideline should be that the total number of hours approximates the total number of hours you currently spend on your business. If you want to increase the amount of time you spend, allow for those extra hours somewhere. Or if you feel the need to scale back on your hours, determine which business activities you can minimize and schedule accordingly.

As business owners, marketing and networking are the most important things we can do to create a thriving enterprise. As you scan your business hours, include time to attend networking events (which can occur at all times of the day and evening, so you may want to pick and choose the ones that best fit your time available). Also, isolate a half-hour to an hour each week to focus on marketing efforts. You will not regret regularly evaluating your marketing strategy, determining what works and what you can try next. Dedicated marketing time can help pinpoint niches and target audiences you hadn't anticipated, or it can help you avoid putting time and energy into efforts that are not paying off.

Along with marketing time, you might want to consider scheduling specific hours each week to complete paperwork and other administrative issues. For many, the administrative aspects of business ownership are not the most fun – and they are more likely to fall to the periphery of our attention. But carving out specific time for the more mundane tasks will indeed increase the chances they will get done. Do consider it.

The beauty of having business hours is that you will be less tempted to steal time from other activities for your business. They will help you reduce multitasking, and give you a higher degree of control over your schedule and your life. If a voice mail comes in, you can say to yourself, "I will respond to it at 1:00 when I am open for business. Until then, I will run household errands and plan for dinner tonight." You can then relax, knowing you have devoted time for business tasks.

You might also consider publicizing your business hours. If you worry about how your clients will perceive you if you wait to respond to their inquiries, you can always tell them your hours on your voice mail message. For example, your message might include wording such as "I return calls between 1:00 and 3:00 PM, Monday through Friday. If these times do not suit you for a return call, please indicate a time and day that might be better. Or feel free to email me at….."

In this way, you inform your clients of the boundaries around your time. If giving specific hours feels too structured, your message could always say something like, "I typically return phone calls within 24 hours of receiving your message. If you need a more speedy response, please let me know, or send me an email." With either case, rest assured that communicating your hours of operation will assist your clients, too. They will know when to expect a return call from you, allowing them to plan accordingly.

The Email Dilemma

By far, the biggest distraction WAHMs encounter is email and the internet. Anything involving a screen seems to eat up time at a faster rate than any other activity known to mankind. "Just checking email" might translate into two hours, thereby reducing the amount of time you have for other things (even sleep!).

Email is a mixed blessing, for sure. It facilitates communication, allowing service and product providers to reach countless numbers of potential customers they otherwise might miss. Effective use of email provides opportunities to advertise and market businesses using signature lines and links to web sites. A customer can ask you one quick question, and you can respond when you have the time, and as in depth as you wish to go. Phone calls take longer and must occur when both people are available for an equal amount of time. While nothing will replace the intimacy of voice to voice interaction, email definitely enhances the frequency and type of communication.

Problems occur when people start to over-utilize email. For many, checking email is the first thing they do when returning home from being away for just a few hours. The pull to check email can be so strong it might feel like a compulsion, fueling a fear that you might be "missing out on something." Some treat email as if it is like phone conversations – you "must" respond to the message the moment it arrives in your inbox, and you "must" check it constantly in order to rapidly reply. While email links us with the outside world, it can also chain us to a screen like an insecure toddler wanting something so badly that they obsess and perseverate on it.

If you have developed an excessive use of email, it might help to understand it as a distraction, a crutch you use to pull you away from something else. Occasionally your chatty toddler might push you over the edge with his non-stop dialogue, so you retreat to email. Or you just feel like a general escape, so you retreat to email. Or you're bored, so you retreat to email. Regardless of the exact reason, email distracts us from all manner of events and situations that demand our time and attention.

The key is to discern the difference between checking email for the sole purpose of communicating information versus for some other reason. If you fall into the category of folks who check email "too much," record possible reasons for your excessive email checking here:

_____
_____
_____
_____
_____
_____
_____

When you establish your hours of operation, include specific time to check email. It can be frequently throughout the day, or can be simply once or twice a day for longer stretches of time. Once you have this in place, you will have to tackle the inevitable urge to check it even during hours you have allotted for other activities. It is during these moments that you can become acutely aware of the role email plays in your life. Ask yourself, "What am I telling myself as I feel that urge to check emails? Where is the discomfort coming from?" Take a few moments to sit with that tension to allow yourself time to process the reasons behind your email fascination. Write your insights here:

Now that you have developed an awareness of what drives your distraction, you can find alternative ways to fill those needs. For instance, perhaps you are generally bored by current events in your life. Maybe your business isn't fulfilling as many areas as you thought it might. Could it be time to find a new hobby? Start that exercise program? Have more family time? Begin planning a summer vacation? Start writing a book?

Or have you uncovered a tendency to avoid things in your life. Why are you avoiding it? What would happen if you engaged with the situation rather than run from it? Can you find a friend or someone to talk to about the situation so you can deal with it from a more healthy perspective?

In the following space, write down alternatives to checking emails to help you cope with your situation.

You can learn to wean yourself away from email. It feels like a relatively benign action, but left unattended, excessive email checking can lead to elevated stress. The issues that are not being dealt with may eventually increase and expand, creating an even bigger stress. But starting now, you can corral your time and attention, moving towards productivity and growth.

What Happened to My Vacation Time???

This is one of those perks we don't think about until about six months into a home-based business. "Where is my vacation time? What happened to my sick days?" Working outside the home, you can take a day off here and there just to decompress, change the scenery, or just do nothing. Being your own boss, there is no mechanism for this. In fact, there is a *disincentive* to take time off!

Unfortunately, we don't get paid sick leave or vacation time. In fact, for many WAHMs, if we don't work, we don't get paid at all. Some WAHMs might have business structures in which they receive some income even when they aren't working, but not everyone has this. Nor is the amount of money as much as normal.

Because WAHMs have no built-in leave time, it becomes extremely important to schedule it in ahead of time. Obviously we can't know in advance when we will be getting sick, but for many of us, we can assume that at some point we will feel under the weather enough to stay in bed all day. Given this inevitability, what plans do you have in place for this situation? How will you accommodate the downtime?

_____
_____
_____
_____
_____

As for vacation and holiday time, make sure you plan for days off on a regular basis. That might mean once a month or once a quarter, but as long as it is regular, expected, and planned for. If you worked for a company and a national holiday came up, you would not be expected to check email or do work on that day. Institute similar "rules" for your holidays and vacations. Make these true breaks from your work. Time apart from the normal schedule is restorative and healthy. Being without it predictably leads to depletion and burn out.

Maybe you just wake up one day and feel like taking the day off. So do it! The world will continue to spin and your business will be there tomorrow. Change the message on your voice mail to let people know that you won't be returning calls until tomorrow, set up an automated email responder saying the same thing, and take off for the hills! Playing hooky once in a while is fun, energizing, and stress reducing. What's stopping you?

What arrangements can you put in place to make it easier to take time off, both scheduled and unscheduled?

_____
_____
_____
_____
_____
_____

The Power in Planning Time

One of the most effective time management techniques you can rather simply introduce is to take about 10 minutes every day and plan for the following day. Many WAHMs use to-do lists, and while they are valuable, the planning time I strongly advocate using goes beyond writing down the tasks.

In addition to listing the tasks you intend to accomplish, take a few extra minutes to gather everything you might need in order to do those tasks. For example, if you have a list of customers you want to call, as well as house-related phone calls to make, find all of the phone numbers you will need the next day and place them next to your to-do list. Having them all in one place will streamline your task when you sit down to make the calls. Leaving that detail until the next day could become a barrier to getting the calls done – if you have to search for something when you are strapped for time, you may end up skipping the call all together. But looking for the number before bedtime when there is less time pressure might make your life easier tomorrow.

Another example is to collect any supplies you will need for various tasks, and place them where you will use them. If you are in the middle of some project, make a brief note on your to-do list about where you left off, and what you will pick up on when you return to that project. This can make a huge difference in projects that you return to more sporadically, where large amounts of time go by before you resume. It saves you the time of refreshing your memory and having to recall what you wanted to do next.

Always include time for exercise and relaxation/meditation!

I also recommend you take your planning time just a bit further, and write out your schedule for the following day, using your business hours as a guideline. Indicate the time you will do each activity, and an approximate amount of time the activity will require. Often, we make the mistake of underestimating how long something will actually take to do. For instance, I have learned over the years that ANYTHING involving the computer (installing or learning new software, transferring file, inputting data) takes at least an hour, maybe two. I used to believe computer issues would only consume 15 minutes at the most (how hard could it be to learn the new software?). Alas, a difficult but valuable lesson.

Having everything you need in one place, along with time allotted for each activity can greatly reduce your stress level. Knowing you have the time and resources to accomplish everything you want to makes an enormous difference in your emotional experience.

At what point in your day would it make sense for you to regularly spend time planning for the next day?

_____
_____
_____

Embrace Delegating!

Starting a new business, even a part time one, creates a new demand on your time. Structuring and planning will help you manage your demands quite nicely, and exercise, relaxation training, and deep breathing will keep you physiologically on track as well. However, at a certain point, we may still struggle with effectively meeting the needs for self care, business care, family care, and home care.

If you reach this juncture, start to delegate. And do it happily! In fact, delegating chores to your children in particular can be one of the most important parenting opportunities you will encounter on a regular basis. Teaching your children how to clean parts of the house, or keep rooms picked up on a regular basis, or take care of the pets provides them valuable life experience that they will use forever. Depending on the ages of your children, they might even have the maturity to absorb some demanding jobs, such as mowing the lawn, cleaning bathrooms, doing laundry, and vacuuming. If you use non-toxic cleaning products, you can even have young children in charge of cleaning the bathroom sinks without worrying about them handling chemicals.

As parents, our job is ultimately to nurture our children into competent, independent adults. While they lack the experience and judgment that come with age, they do have brain power that adults often overlook. That means that your children are likely capable of doing more around the house than they might currently do. You will still have to "police" their work, and may have to remind them repeatedly to actually *do* the chores. But they will be done by someone other than you, using a method that will benefit them as adults. Although they might not initially appreciate this gift you are giving them!

More opportunities for delegating exist beyond your children. Asking your husband to chip in more with specific duties could help. Some men are reluctant to do more household chores than they currently perform. Whether requesting more assistance from a husband or from children, specifying an exact duty helps enhance compliance. If you approach this issue with the statement, "I really need more help around here," you will likely elicit a vague, "OK, I'll see what I can do to help." Don't be surprised if nothing actually materializes. While you have a whole list of possible tasks they could do, they probably have no real clue about what needs to be done.

Direct requests will get better results. A question like, "Would you be able to empty the dishwasher every morning before you go to work?" may have less resistance. The job is a relatively small, precise one. It would be easier to agree to take this on as opposed to a more general, "Could you clean the kitchen?"

Is the idea of roping your family into more household chores daunting? Some women assume the effort it will require just to convince their family to do these things outweighs the time saved. Indeed, it might take more energy in the short term to have them pull more weight around the house. However, you will not regret expending that effort in the long run.

But change is difficult for people to cope with, particularly change they didn't expect or ask for. Do prepare for some backlash, and even irritation from family members. One of the best ways to counteract this unpleasantness and help husbands and children accept their new roles more easily is to approach managing your WAHM lifestyle as the CEO of a company would. Successful leaders do many things well, but one of the most effective methods they use is getting everyone in the group to buy into a common vision. That means they develop a vision for their operation that is compelling and exciting, and then they constantly remind their workers of that vision. The leader then points out how each employee's efforts help propel the group as a whole towards creating that vision. As a result, every worker feels better about what they do, because they have a clear understanding of how their specific job impacts the big picture.

As the leader of your WAH life, you can utilize this same tactic. You and your husband might work on developing a vision for your family, including everything from his career, to your business, to the children's education, to yearly vacations. Then, call a family meeting in which you and your husband can paint a picture of the vision you hold for your family. Explain why you choose particular goals and ideas, and then describe how each family member needs to do their own part in order to get the family where you want to be. This might mean taking on more cleaning or yard duties, babysitting younger children, or even scaling back on excessive extra-curricular activities. It will especially help children understand how critical their participation is if you explicitly state, "Now that you will be in charge of filling and emptying the dishwasher, I can take those extra 15 minutes every day to make phone calls to get more clients for my business. When I reach my goal of 20 new clients, the family can take a short vacation as a reward!" Not only will this approach eventually reduce some of your stress, it can bring your family together in important ways.

Also, roping everyone together towards a common goal can reduce possible resentment that a spouse or child may feel towards the mother's job. Many of my clients have mentioned that their husbands feel bitter towards their jobs because it means changing the way things are done around the house (translation: husbands have to do more). Children sometimes feel this way, too.

But helping them all understand that each member of the family contributes to the functioning of the whole provides them with more meaning and fulfillment. They know that their chores have significance and consequence for the entire family. And over time, as a WAHM, you teach them the power of business ownership and how team work makes it happen. Eventually your children might even be able to help you with paperwork, inventory, carrying supplies, or other business-related duties. That is an education that even the best school districts can't provide.

Delegating to family members makes intuitive sense. But if family members are already overloaded, or if for some other reason it is not feasible for them to help, delegation can come in other forms. Hiring household help for cleaning and minor repairs can alleviate much pressure. Or having a lawn service handle mowing, trimming, and general weeding frees up tons of time. Certainly the cost factor needs to be considered. If it is too costly for regular house cleaning or lawn work, think about more creative ways of using their services. Perhaps have your house professionally cleaned once every three months. You will still have to maintain your cleaning, but having someone do a thorough job every once in a while can really help.

For lawn work, perhaps hire a neighborhood teenager to mow. If that expense is too much, again see if the teen would agree to mow once a month. It will not eliminate the need for you do it, but can relieve some of the responsibility.

In business-related tasks, research the use of Virtual Assistants. VA's are people whose business it is to offer administrative (or other) support to other businesses using the internet, fax, and other forms of technology. I know of quite a few business owners who utilize the services of a VA and would be lost without them! The need for VA's grew in large part to the growth of WAH businesses (both men and women). These businesses often need part time or inconsistent administrative support, and hiring a permanent employee is too burdensome. In some cases, a business owner operating out of her home might not feel comfortable having an employee physically in the house with her. Also, she might not have enough work to guarantee the return on investment of hiring an assistant.

With the trend towards virtual everything, people began to realize the flexibility of offering many services to specifically support the WAH business model. You can hire a VA to help with just one thing, or with many things, for just a one time job, or a consistent and permanent job. For example, if you have standard emails or snail mailings you send to new clients, or to existing clients on a regular basis, you can send them to your VA and have her/him actually send them out on your behalf whenever you want. So each time you get a new client, you notify your VA and that person handles all of your new client chores. Each VA might have their own restrictions, so it is necessary to research and ask questions. But the availability and convenience of a VA is highly worthwhile!

Now that I have mentioned many ways to think about delegating responsibilities, take a few moments to consider the various opportunities you have to reduce your stress by shedding some chores. Record your thoughts here:

_____
_____
_____
_____

_____
_____
_____
_____

Do you want to approach your life as an effective leader would? Write your vision for your life here, and then share it with your husband. Modify it accordingly, and then have a family meeting in which you will tell your children of this vision, and how they can help the family move towards it. Or, have the children participate in crafting the family vision – it will increase their overall commitment if they are part of the visioning process!

Write out your initial vision here, and then record any thoughts you have about including the family in achieving the vision.

_____
_____
_____
_____
_____
_____
_____
_____
_____
_____

Chapter 9 – Seeing the Results

Finally you have arrived at the end of this workbook! Hopefully you have completed some of the exercises and suggestions along the way, and have experienced at least a little relief from stress.

I presented quite a bit of information, as well as many suggestions on how to adjust aspects of your life to relieve some pressure. Some of these changes are easier to make, and others require more time, effort, and energy to implement. I will reiterate – the beauty of having this book in your hands is that you can return to it over and over, trying different things at different times.

The fact is that some techniques will help you more than others at various points in your life. Now that you have gone through this book, you have a sense of the types of actions you can take as your life evolves.

Just to review, I have addressed the physical aspects of stress and how they can impact your health (Chapter 2). Using breathing and relaxation techniques, along with regular exercise, you can learn to mediate the effects of stress on your well being (Chapter 5).

Also, you learned about how we ultimately "create" our own stress in our minds by the self talk we use (Chapter 6). Adapting alternate ways of looking at events in your life will help you manage stress by allowing you to diminish the perceived severity of those events.

When important people in our lives fail to respect our home based businesses, examining how we project our business-attitude can shed some light on this challenging scenario (Chapter 7). Opening lines of communication and discovering the thoughts and concerns that others have regarding your home based business can advance understanding and acceptance.

And finally, time management skills and schedule re-organization can streamline and focus your daily, weekly, and monthly activities (Chapter 8). This will have a direct impact not only on your business, but on your home life and self-care activities as well.

With all of this knowledge under your belt, what can you expect now? At this point, I would encourage you to return to Chapter 4 and your vision of your ideal life. You have the freedom and power to determine how much you want to achieve that vision. How many changes are you able and willing to make right now in order to inch ever closer to your ideal life?

Even when you achieve your ideal life, you might find you still feel a bit discontented. Does this shock you? It often surprises people when they work so hard to achieve something they really want, but discover it isn't enough. This phenomenon occurs because the process of making fundamental changes in our lives initiates learning and growth. Maturation causes us to re-evaluate that which we believed to be important in the past. Therefore, our vision might need to be "tweaked" to account for this personal growth.

I would be remiss if I failed to mention the almost inevitable need to change and shift as you move forward. The fact is that your business will change with time, your children will grow and their needs will change, you will get older and gain perspective and insight, and your relationships will evolve. All of this change means that your stress relief efforts will also need to adjust.

I strongly encourage you to see stress as something to be relieved, not eliminated. Although a "stress-free" life sounds appealing, it really is not. A certain amount of stress is not only normal and desirable, but will also result in better performance in life. Think back to when you were in school and you had a big exam the next day. If you felt no stress or pressure about it, would you have felt compelled to study at all? Probably not! Of course, too much stress will result in worse performance. The ultimate goal is to find that "sweet spot" in which you label the pressure you feel as "motivation," and not stress.

Your life is dynamic. Even without specific, life-altering events (like having another child), the needs and requirements of people around you will fluctuate. Then there are the (ahem....) inevitable changes that happen to our bodies with the passage of time. Therefore, self-care activities must grow with those changes.

I mention all of this to drive home the point that, because life happens, stress relief efforts must constantly be re-evaluated. Even if you do every single thing in this book, you would not be able to sit back on your bum and say, "There, now stress is managed and my life is balanced." Relieving stress and seeking life balance are ongoing. Balance is not a state of being, but rather a way of life.

Now, fresh with the knowledge in this book, you have everything you need in order to meet this challenge! It means you can continually refine, or even radically alter your vision and be able to attain it.

The payoff can be enormous – a life that fulfills you in the most important and meaningful ways. What more could you ask for?

Good luck!

[107]

www.ingramcontent.com/pod-product-compliance
Ingram Content Group UK Ltd.
Pitfield, Milton Keynes, MK11 3LW, UK
UKHW051524180426
11947UKWH00018B/1555